A World of Earrings

Anne van Cutsem

A World of Earrings

Africa, Asia, America
from the Ghysels Collection

Photos by
Mauro Magliani

Translation by Judith Landry

SKIRA

Scientific Editor
Eric Ghysels

Art Director
Marcello Francone

Editorial Coordination
Marzia Branca

Editing
Claudio Nasso, Enza Sicuri

Layout
Serena Parini

The publisher thanks the Ghysels family
for allowing the publication of their collection,
and in particular Colette Ghysels
for the composition of the pictures and the
cooperation with the layout.

The earrings are reproduced in their real size,
except those on pages 33, 60, 93, 146, 209 and 212.
When in one picture appear more than one earring,
the sizes indicated refer to the bigger one.

First published in Italy in 2001 by
Skira Editore S.p.A.
Palazzo Casati Stampa
via Torino 61
20123 Milano
Italy

© 2001 Skira editore, Milano

Printed and bound in Italy. First edition

ISBN 88-8118-973-9

Distributed in North America and Latin America
by Rizzoli International Publications, Inc.
through St. Martin's Press,
175 Fifth Avenue, New York, NY 10010.
Distributed elsewhere in the world
by Thames and Hudson Ltd.,
181a High Holborn, London WC1V 7QX,
United Kingdom

Contents

A Matter of Seduction?

When we look at the outline of a head, our gaze is immediately drawn towards the face, framed by the earrings. Hoops, rings, studs, cylinders, discs, pendants, earplugs, temple ornaments … earrings come in every shape and size.

The original purpose of earrings was protective rather than ornamental: as natural openings, ears, and the auditory canal, are threatened by intrusive spirits. The rim, outer ear and lobe may be pierced in many places. As the seat of hearing, the ear enables man to fend off the dangers of the bush and forest. Lastly, the ear is the vehicle for aural knowledge, vital to peoples who do not transmit information through the written word.

Since the earliest times, earrings have served as accessories to seduction, and craftsmen all over the world have unleashed their imagination to create them, using the most varied materials: those of their natural environments, first and foremost, with the use of flowers and grasses, horn and feathers, wood, shells and ivory, and the stones and metals they found in lodes and alluvial deposits. Adventurous caravaneers and sailors set out in search of further exotic materials.

At first, techniques were rudimentary, though they required dexterity and expertise. The polishing and piercing of stones and shells is an arduous process. The earliest gold was hammered into shape, so was the wire. Then goldsmiths began to cast their models in sand, or by the lost wax process. Forms were further enriched by *repoussé* work, and chasing. Filigree and granulation are due to the continuous refinement of the soldering technique. As a finishing touch, metal might be nielloed, enamelled and stone mounted. Westerners have used the term "barbarian" to describe those being "benighted" enough to follow customs different from their own; yet clearly there are no "geographical savages", only men whose wealth of differences must be respected[1]. For the Kikuyu of Kenya, the wearing of numerous ear ornaments entitles them to respect, as long as the ear lobes are not torn[2]. The statues of Buddha, the enlightened one, show him with very long ears.

Seeking the truth through asceticism, he renounced the emblems of his rank, which included heavy gold ear pendants, and his distended lobes have thus become a symbol of wisdom.

Offered as gifts by the family of the suitor in the Indonesian archipelagos, earrings serve to seal the union; among the Masai, ear flaps of beaded leather proclaim the status of the married woman. Worn by men in the Philippines and among the Naga headhunters, ear ornaments tell of their prowess in war and hunting.

Generally speaking, earrings are worn in pairs, particularly by women. In Tibet men often wear just a single earring or two of differing type. In this work, only one earring of pairs will be sometimes shown, thus allowing space to illustrate more types of earrings.

Most of the ornaments illustrated here date from the nineteenth and twentieth centuries; however, earrings found during archaeological excavations bear striking witness to the ancient origins of their motifs, and their durability over time. Globalisation, with its attendant cultural attrition, has caused many types to fall into disuse. In many places, a period of rapid decline began as early as the post-war period; nonetheless some earrings dating from that time, or even later, may be regarded as having cultural merit, provided they have been made by the peoples who wear them, or have been incorporated into their culture and are generally worn.

Their travels through time and space inspired the Ghysels family with a passion for collecting, among others, earrings. Jean-Pierre is interested in sculptural forms; Colette's magpie imagination has led her to be also captivated by unusual and baroque objects. Later, their interests were inherited by their sons Marc, Eric and David.

The collection presented here reveals an abiding concern for quality and beauty, and a taste for variations on a theme; in this lies its particular interest and appeal. Museum collections, on the other hand, have to be didactic, thus typological, they are not built up over the course of a lifetime.

[1] Roy, *Arts Sauvages*, p. 7.
[2] Borel, *op. cit.*, p. 80.

Africa

The continent of Africa has always been a land of migration, with the influence of foreign cultures playing an important part; even those regions which have experienced few population upheavals have been visited by traders bringing with them new wares, materials and techniques. Their contributions have been absorbed, and sometimes adapted, according to the degree of open-mindedness and technological capabilities of those involved. Glass beads imported from Europe were hugely popular in Africa: apart from their attractive colours, they were also easy to use, offering an alternative to the far more laborious process of collecting seeds, or making metal beads. Similarly, wire was a convenient alternative to grasses and vegetable fibres, which are delicate by nature.

With the adoption of such imported materials, the original meaning of these jewels was often lost, though their purely formal or decorative values might be enhanced. Decorations, which look purely geometrical, are in fact abstractions: a lozenge may represent the scales of a serpent, chevrons may be a reference to water.

A new owner may also modify the initial function of an object: a safety pin may be metamorphosed into an earring in Kenya, and a cartridge case or a tack may be used to decorate an earplug in central Africa.

The custom of ear piercing, which dates back to the Stone Ages, serves as a means of protection, for decoration, or for the display of some prestigious object, such as a snuff box or an object of acculturation such as a button.

When worn by a woman, earrings serve above all as ornament, though they also convey information concerning her status, whether single, married, mother or widow. When worn by a man, they emphasise his role as chief or dignitary, or indicate his prowess, by means of hunting trophies worn suspended from the ears. In white Africa, earrings are a female attribute; in black Africa, the situation varies from tribe to tribe.

The Maghreb

Before the Arab conquest, finished in the eighth century, the indigenous Berber population of northwest Africa was subject to a variety of influences, with those of the Mediterranean cultures predominating throughout antiquity. From the fifth century B.C. onwards, they traded with the Phoenicians – exceptional sailors who founded colonies from Cyprus to Spain – and the Carthaginians, while Rome and Byzantium maintained an armed presence. Then came the barbarous Visigoth invaders, whose influence is reflected in earrings from Fez, with similarities to medieval European jewels. Baroque jewels from Andalusia and Ottoman Turkey also exerted an influence on North African craftsmen.

Theocentric Islam was then superimposed upon the formal language characteristic of the Berbers: with varying degrees of regional intensity, its decisive mark explains a family likeness throughout the region. Large hoops and temple ornaments are a typically Arab feature, as is the use of an abundance of little chains ending in pendants in the form of the hand of Fatima, or a crescent moon.

Earrings are the jewels most worn by the women of the Maghreb, and girl's ears are pierced at a very young age. As women like to wear several pieces at a time, the external ear too must be pierced. In the past a married woman from Annaba, in Algeria, might wear eight pairs of earrings of various shapes and with various names[1].

In the Maghreb, there are two very distinct styles of ornament: one worn exclusively by women who live in towns, richer and more influenced by Arab culture, with gold jewels, sometimes enhanced with precious stones; and one worn by Berber countrywomen, who love forcefully shaped silver ornaments, sometimes heightened by glassware, coral, enamel or niello.

Earrings also speak a symbolic language. Despite their apparent diversity, what such symbols have in common is a link with the idea of life: fertility and fecundity are essential to human existence, and survival. The natural elements – sky and water – and the stars – sun and moon – are often alluded to. For fear of idolatry, Islam forbids the representation of living beings, giving preference to geometrical figures and more abstract allusions, such as Arabic numerals.

One single jewel may often lend itself to several levels of symbolic interpretation, concerning its material – silver, as a symbol of purity – its form – the crescent, the emblem of Islam – and its engraved decoration – the fish, a portent of fertility because of the large number of eggs it lays.

Morocco

According to Rachel Hasson, no fewer than four hundred and eighty tribes have been known to live in Morocco[2]: as signs of tribal identity, jewels, and earrings in particular, are therefore highly diversified. Those of the Anti- Atlas are strikingly profuse and sumptuous; among the most spectacular are the headdress pendants with further disc-shaped or lozenge-shaped pendants, from Tamanart (p. 23), and the *tiboukaria* with enamelled serpents' heads (p. 29). The magical powers of the serpent are alluded to in legends dating back to antiquity: the mother of Scipio Africanus was barren until the day a serpent was seen at her side. The Ida ou Nadif make nielloed *tikhoursin ouguelmin* which may be either trapezoid or crescent-shaped (pp. 24-25). The Jewish craftsmen of Tahala make splendid enamelled hoops (p. 17), whose inner motif represents a dove's foot. The symbol of love because of its gentle ways, and also of purity, because of its spotless whiteness[3], the dove is the bird most frequently represented.

A cultural legacy from its Byzantine and Visigoth past, enamel and niello were particularly prized in Spain, together with the setting of stones. The dynasties of the Almoravids and Almohads (1091–1237) extended their rule to both shores of the Mediterranean, and thus Andalusian culture penetrated the Maghreb, while the gradual Christian reconquest of the Islamic kingdom of Spain caused many Jewish and Muslim families to emigrate to north Africa. The Inquisition set off a new wave of immigration, and the pressure exerted by the new arrivals sent some families moving down to the Anti-Atlas, where goldsmiths opened up new workshops[4].

Algeria

In rural Algeria every woman, whatever her social rank, owns at least one pair of earrings and one pair of bracelets for everyday use, and more elaborate sets for festive occasions. The amassing of jewels begins in earliest infancy, when the little girl is given a pair of earrings and a pair of bracelets, while she acquires a jewel when she makes her first fast. The parents of her future husband offer her ornaments for the engagement and on religious celebrations, and her own parents complete the collection when the marriage takes place. A mother gives her daughter ornaments that she herself has been given by her own mother; family jewels are handed down solely from mother to daughter[5].

On her wedding day, resplendent in her finery, the young woman's lustre reflects on her entire family; furthermore, she has now attained a new social status. From now on, each key event in her life will be marked by the acquisition of a jewel, with the resulting collection remaining her own property, a reserve to be drawn upon in times of scarcity.

The splendours of the medieval North African cities emerge in all their glory in the accounts of Arab writers, worthy rivals to Baghdad and Cordova; they were also renowned for their embroidered fabrics and goldsmithing. In 1492, the fall of Granada led to the Spanish occupation of various coastal areas; the Muslim population appealed to the Turks to come to the rescue, and Charles V was compelled to retreat from just outside Algiers. The gold jewels worn by town-dwellers, heightened with precious stones and baroque pearls, imply a desire for self-aggrandisement. Thus Andalusian and Turkish influences were grafted on to a Berber substratum, characterised by geometrical forms.

In Kabylia – situated in the mountain massifs which form part of the Tell Atlas bordering the Mediterranean, and dotted with small villages perched on rocky peaks – the most famous goldsmiths are found among the Beni Yenni. Unlike other regions of North Africa, here the craft is practised by Jews and Muslims alike. Indeed, in the middle of the nineteenth century, certain tribes prevented Jews from entering their territory for fear of competition[6]. When a craftsman had no son to whom to pass down the secrets of his trade, he would turn to his wife and daughters.

Silver is the basic material used for earrings, and is obtained by the melting down in a crucible of coins or jewels that are old and damaged or discarded. There is often a presence of coral and enamel elements (p. 30).

When a woman gets married, she puts on all the jewellery she has received so far; hereafter she will wear it at important family gatherings, or at religious and spring festivals. For everyday purposes she may do with a pair of earrings, bracelets, and a necklace. During periods of mourning she wears no jewels[7].

The Romans were the only conquerors ever able to overcome the resistance put up by the inhabitants of the Aures mountains. Filigree, granulation and openwork piercing, or *opus interrasile*, themselves borrowed from the Romans, are the techniques which characterise local workmanship.

The Byzantine army, headed by Belisarius, drove out the Vandals in 533, and their taste for opulence gradually also made its mark on the Berber elite. We have reason to believe that their goldsmiths were acquainted with certain types of Byzantine jewels: *timsarfin* earrings, in the form of a hoop open at one end, with openwork decoration, are strikingly similar to Byzantine examples.

Earrings are particularly popular as an everyday ornament with the women of Chaouen. Other head ornaments, such as diadems and temple ornaments, are worn on feast days[8]. Widows replace their earrings with a white thread[9].

At the menopause, the women of the Aures replace the *bularwah*, the "soul bearer" which they have worn since puberty, with the more fitting *imehriyen*, a simple silver ring decorated with a horn sphere, a custom which bears out the sexual connotation of the earring in north Africa[10].

The traditional types found in the Aures are not peculiar to this region; some are found throughout rural Algeria, made by Jewish craftsmen who have settled in the big towns. In the past, hoops, partly hidden by the headdress, might measure as much as fifteen centimetres in diameter, and women wore two or three pairs at a time, their weight being lightened by a thread running over the head. Rosette pendants are held in place by a number of very long chains (p. 31); made up of round intertwined hoops, they end in little crescent-shaped drop earrings.

Tunisia

Every Tunisian woman, of whatever age, in town and country alike, wears earrings, though they vary from place to place in shape and material, in the way the elements are assembled, and in motif and technique.

Every woman owns a certain number of jewels which have been given her by her fiancé and family. If she does not have enough, she may borrow others, in order to be resplendent on her wedding day, the key moment of her life.

The dowry given her by her fiancé is made up of the *nakd*, a sum of money and a quantity of food stuffs, and of the *mlak*, consisting of clothing and jewels. These goods become her property. However, if she is divorced as a result of her own misconduct, she must return the jewels to her husband. The dowry has not just an economic value, but also a symbolic one, entitling the husband to intimate relations with his wife. The settlement varies in value according to whether the bride is a virgin, a divorcee or a widow[11].

Hoops are found throughout the country, while rings are essentially for city wear; the hoops are made of gold, or medium and small in size in the towns, of silver, and larger in size, in country areas. Silvergilt jewels, such as the temple ornaments known as *qandila* (p. 33), hanging on the headdress of brides in Djerba, reveal the influence of western Islam, originating in Andalusia[12].

Jews arrived in Djerba after the first destruction of the Temple in Jerusalem in 586 B.C.; they converted a number of Berbers, who then resisted the first Arab conquests in the seventh century, as we know from the writings of the fourteenth-century Arab historian and philosopher, Ibn Khaldun.

In large cities such as Tunis, Bizerte and Kairouan, the techniques are more sophisticated and the metals more precious. As the capital of the Hafsid dynasty, Tunis had a jewellers' souq as early as the thirteenth century. Conquered by Charles V in 1535, it was retaken some twenty years later by the Ottomans, and remained the capital both under them and during the French protectorate. Thus Tunis has been a cosmopolitan city for centuries, a meeting place for rulers and ambassadors who constantly exchanged gifts, including jewels. As a port, Tunis was also the recipient of merchandise from both East and West, and, as such, had considerable importance and exerted great influence. The costumes and jewels of the women of Tunis inspired those of the women of Bizerte, Kairouan and Sfax.

Ever since antiquity, the coastal area has been dotted with towns and villages where the main centres of jewellery making developed. The coastal area is a melting-pot for the cultures of north Africa, the Mediterranean and the Arab-Muslim world.

The western region of Tunisia, on the other hand, consists mainly of small country villages, with no centre for jewellery making. Women wear earrings modelled on those of neighbouring Algeria, such as those of the Aures and the area around Constantine.

The hoops worn in the southern towns of Medenine and Tataouine are remarkable both for their quality, their fine silver, and their strikingly dynamic forms (p. 37).

Until independence, the art of jewellery making was practised almost exclusively by Jews. The various crafts, brought together in *souqs* in the heart of the old *medina*, were originally divided up into guilds represented by an *amine*, who acted as an intermediary between the authorities and the professional bodies, playing an administrative, economic and judicial role[13].

The Tuareg

Referred to as Tuareg by outsiders, their own name for themselves is *Imohar*, free men; they may also refer to themselves by the name of the region where they live or by that of their tribe. The women's only head ornament – apart from their elaborately plaited hair – is their striking silver earrings, engraved with abstract geometrical motifs. Silversmiths frequently sign their work at the base of the polyhedron, adding the names of the owner. Like the women of North Africa, Targuia wear earrings in pairs (p. 41), out of a desire for symmetry, which also emerges in their bracelets and anklets. Until the last decades, gold was never used, being a feared metal, a superstition not shared by the inhabitants of Black Africa.

Sub-Saharan Africa

In Black Africa, creativity reigns supreme. The head, the seat of thought and the life force, is the object of particular attention: a variety of deformations, scarifications, face painting and assorted piercing are normal practice as protection against demonic forces. Various ethnic groups in Kenya stretch their ear lobes until they touch their shoulders.

Ear ornaments and hairstyles – which are astonishingly varied – are closely linked. Hair is dressed with an eye to seduction, but the hairstyle also provides information as to tribal origins, age and rank. It may also have magical connotations: in order to increase their life force, the Suk of Kenya add the hair of a dead member of their family to their own. Similarly, "horned" hairstyles based on animal horns are frequently found.

Having remained in close contact with his environment, the Black African naturally makes frequent use of materials from the plant world, drawing inspiration from wood, seeds, fruits and grasses. The Bantu rarely use flowers as ornaments, though the pygmy women of the Ituri put sweet-smelling flowers in their ear lobes when they are dancing[14]. Seeds are used by various peoples because of their apotropaic qualities. Certain materials have specific associations: because of its durability, wood suggests strength, and earplugs in the wood of various species, sometimes sweet-smelling, are widely found. Elephant ivory suggests the idea of courage, and ear ornaments in ivory are generally the prerogative of chiefs and their relatives, or of hunters and warriors. A hunter whose ears are adorned with ivory will not only command respect, but will also seek to appease the soul of the elephant he has killed, out of fear of its vengeance[15]. In many places, ivory is more highly valued than gold. Ear ornaments may also be made of bone and horn: the buffalo, a formidable animal, is associated with the idea of power. Giraffe hair, and elephant hide, less appealing in appearance, are frequently used as supports, proving that on occasions the symbolic aspect takes precedence over the decorative effect. Clearly, the animal kingdom exerts enormous fascination, inspiring fear, together with admiration for its beauty and the ease with which it adapts itself to its environment.

With the exception of the empire of the Monomotapa – famous for its stone ruins in Zimbabwe – and the East Coast, the use of noble metals is limited to the regions situated to the north of the Equator. The Wolof women of Senegal, much admired for their beauty, wear their jewels set off against wonderfully becoming boubous and turbans. They also wear pear-shaped ornaments, grouped to one side of the head, or arranged symmetrically, and ear pendants (p. 43), whose filigree and granulation are quite outstanding. Over the centuries, continued contact with Arab traders, leading caravans laden with gold to the Mediterranean over tracks through the Sahara, familiarised local goldsmiths with their sophisticated techniques. In the fifteenth century, in their attempts to penetrate this fabulously wealthy continent, the Portuguese sold jewels to the Wolof, whose own jewellery was subsequently inspired by them.

Medieval Arabic texts mention twisted gold *wangara* earrings, probably dating back to the first millennium AD. The wealth of the empires of Ghana and Mali was based on their trade in gold, using the resources provided by the gold-bearing seams at their disposal.

In 1797 and 1798, Mungo Park mentions gold earrings which he describes as "massy and inconvenient [...] commonly so heavy as to pull down and lacerate the lobe of the ear; to avoid which, they are supported by a thong of red leather, which passes over the crown of the head from one ear to the other."[16] The photographs of the Peul women, from Djenne and Mopti, outstandingly dignified and elegant, with the most beautiful features, are well-known. The better-off among them wear huge earrings (pp. 44-45), which are light despite their considerable size. The making of such quadrilobate ornaments, hammered out of a cruciform gold ingot, requires enormous skill; Peul goldsmiths may have learned their craft from the Songhay[17]. The men offer these earrings to their women after a successful deal at the cattle market, the women may also receive them as a legacy on the death of their own mother.

The Peul also wear superb twisted gold hoops known as *kwoteneje kange* (p. 46). The poorer wear strikingly effective imitations in painted terracotta, beeswax or straw steeped in henna, known as "Timbuktu gold". Women often wear several pairs of earrings in solid silver or bronze, both smooth and twisted, decorated with cornelian or copal, which they hang from their ears, incorporate into their elaborate headdress, or use to decorate their foreheads.

Both men and women insert plugs, discs, chains, shaped wire and above all a large variety of hoops into their ear lobes. Small wooden or ivory rods are fixed into the external ear, and a number of little rings around its rim; the latter may also be attached by pincer-like devices, as is customary among the Sarakole (p. 51). Beyond the Sahel, copper and brass are preferred. In Ghana, gold dust was once exchanged for copper[18].

East Africa

In the lake region of East Africa, following sweeping migratory movements, Nilots, Hamites and Bantu, of various races and cultures, gradually interbred and underwent each others' mutual influence. Kenya offers the widest range of ear ornaments, some of them quite astounding. Society was formerly governed by order of seniority, though the post-war years have witnessed a process of radical upheaval.

Struck by the rapid rate of change, and alarmed at the possibility of the whole loss of an entire tradition, Joy Adamson set out to make water-colour portraits of the tribes in question, though her work met with hostility from certain civil servants, as well as missionaries, who feared that it might give new impetus to customs which were better stamped out in the name of progress and morality. She also had trouble convincing the native chiefs of the advisability of going along with her project, since those being portrayed might fear that, by capturing their images, the painter was thereby imprisoning their souls.

Captivated by the beauty and diversity of the body arts of the peoples of Africa, in the seventies Angela Fisher set off to photograph the various tribes of Kenya; her magnificent photographs show the changes which took place over a mere two decades.

The Nandi and Masai belong to Kenya's main Nilo-Hamitic group. They have a number of customs in common, and wear similar ornaments, including ones in shaped brass wire, and small copper double-cone earrings. Puberty, marriage and the attaining of the status of elder are all stages marked by rituals, accompanied by the giving of accessories. Girls and boys insert ivory rods into their ears to prevent spirits from entering. Girls also wear large beaded rings in the rim of the ear, which they make themselves, as well as those for the boys. The large ornament in carved ivory (p. 53), worn by warriors, seems to have become obsolete since the beginning of the twentieth century. Married women, whose heads are shaved, wear distinctive leather ear flaps (p. 54), decorated with multi-coloured beads imported from Europe. The Masai associate blue beads with God, since they are the colour of His abode, the sky; green beads are suggestive of the vegetation after rain[19].

After excision, Pokot women go into a period of retreat during which they are initiated into the rules of married life, and do not wear any jewellery. On their return to society they adorn themselves with large brass hoops, indicating their nubile status.

Kurya men and women both have very distended ear lobes. The girls wear a huge wooden plug in one single lobe, and ivory discs in the rim. Boys wear extraordinary ornaments in the form of a sort of wooden roller, weighing up to eight pounds, held in place by the two lobes, in front or behind, at shoulder height[20]. The lobes of warriors and hunters are stretched down to their collarbones by the weight of ornaments in brass wire, bent into the shape of a cylinder.

Turkana men are very partial to aluminium (p. 51), which they use in preference to iron for the conical studs and hoops, from which the elders used to hang many little chains. Young girls attach a large number of rods to the rim of their ears.

South Africa

In the nineteenth century, the Zulu had their ears pierced before puberty; carried out either at the new or the full moon, this rite marked the transition from childhood to adulthood. They wore small or medium sized earplugs in terracotta, horn, bone and ivory, and even snuff boxes. Around 1920, larger slightly convex wooden plugs became the fashion. sometimes decorat-

ed with brass tacks. One or two decades later, openwork or painted earplugs began to be made in lighter wood.

Mosaics made of synthetic materials, glued on to softwood plugs, appeared at the end of the 1920s; thanks to the invention of vinyl, more complex motifs appeared around 1950, whose style, with its coloured geometrical forms, is unique in Africa, and more reminding the Amerindians from the south-west of the United States (pp. 8 and 59). Most are made by Zulu craftsmen from Johannesburg; their colours, similar to those of beaded ornaments, are a vehicle for the same symbolic language, while certain series of colour refer to the stage their wearer has reached in the life cycle[21].

[1] Benouniche, *Bijoux et parures d'Algérie*, p. 3.
[2] Hasson, *Schmuck der islamischen Welt*, p. 37.
[3] Chevalier, Gheerbrant, *Dictionnaire des Symboles*, p. 269.
[4] Grammet, in *Splendeurs du Maroc*, p. 216.
[5] Benouniche, *op.cit.*, p. 13.

[6] Camps-Fabrer, *Bijoux berbères d'Algérie*, p. 17.
[7] Camps-Fabrer, *op. cit.*, p. 57.
[8] Benfoughal, *Bijoux et bijoutiers de l'Aurès*, p. 114.
[9] Tamzali, *Abzim. Parures et bijoux des femmes d'Algérie*, p. 43.
[10] Chevalier, Gheerbrant, *op. cit.*, p. 142.

[11] Gargouri-Sethom, *Le bijou traditionnel en Tunisie*, p. 73-6.
[12] Sugier, *Symboles et bijoux traditionnels en Tunisie*, p. 18.
[13] Gargouri-Sethom, *op. cit.*, p. 125.
[14] Leuzinger, *Wesen und Form des Schmuckes afrikanisher Völker*, p. 25.

[15] Leuzinger, *op. cit.*, p. 77.
[16] Quoted in Garrard, *Or d'Afrique*, p. 22.
[17] Garrard, *op. cit.*, p. 32.
[18] Leuzinger, *op. cit.*, p. 36.
[19] Fisher, *Africa adorned*, p. 26.
[20] Adamson, *The Peoples of Kenya*, p. 188.
[21] Jolles, in *Zulu Treasures*, p. 17.

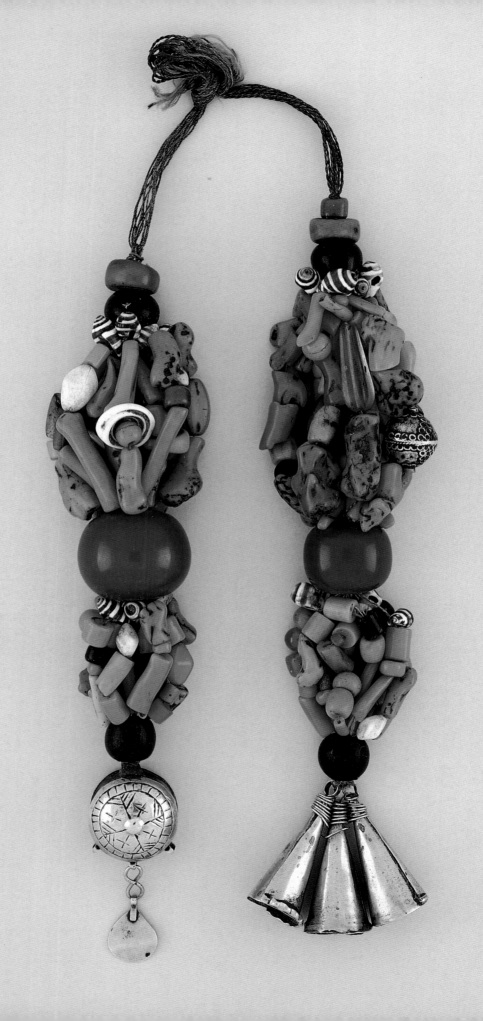

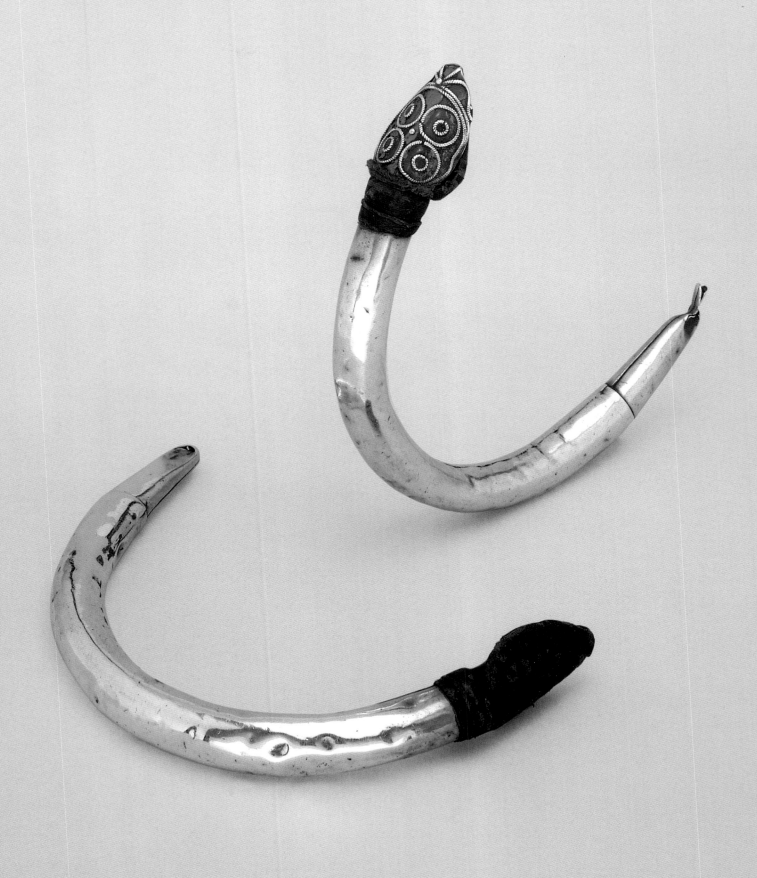

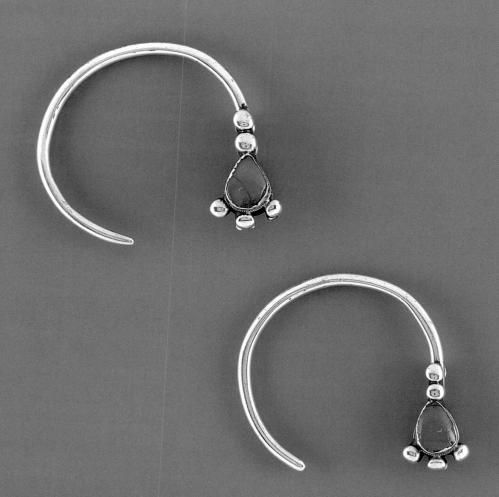

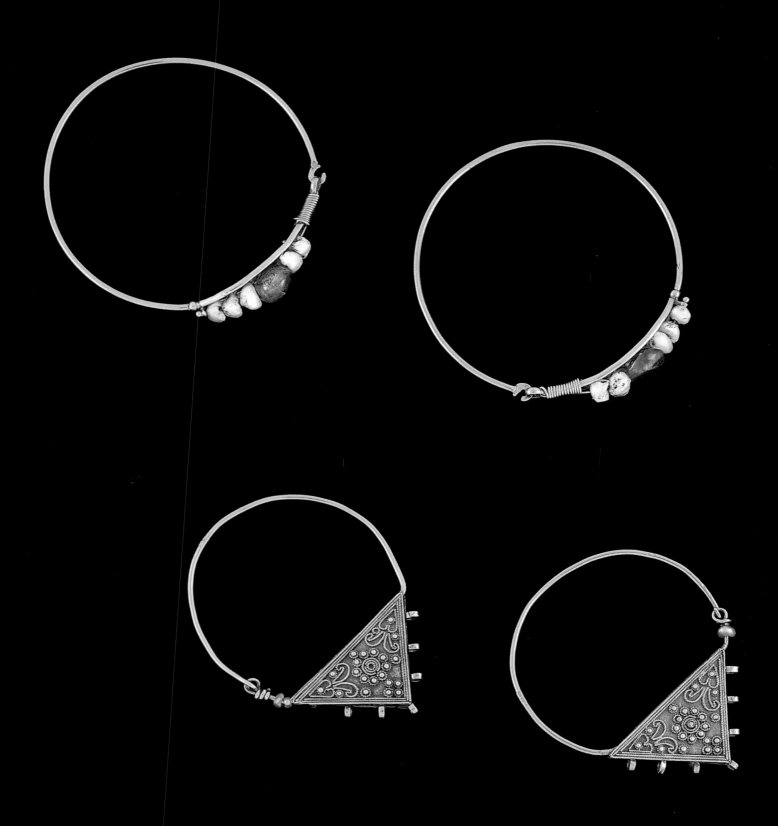

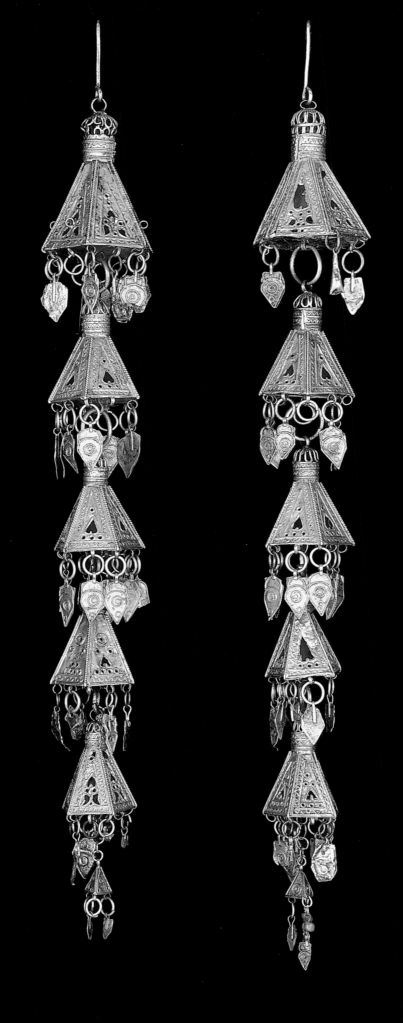

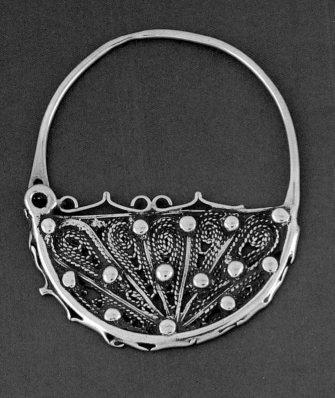

36

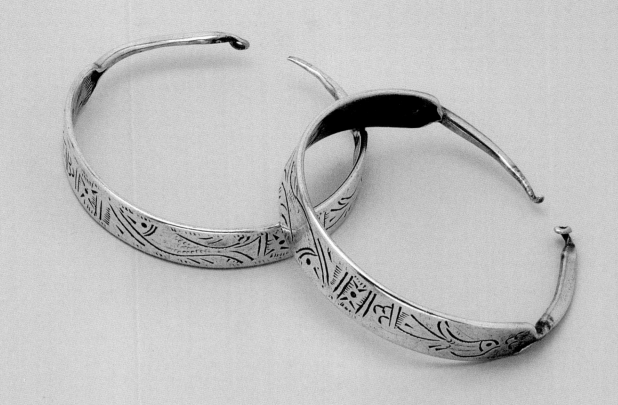

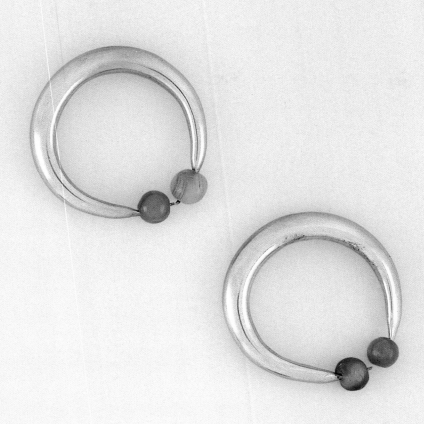

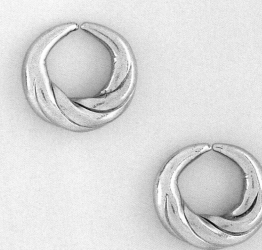

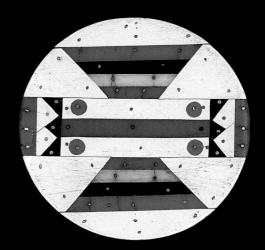
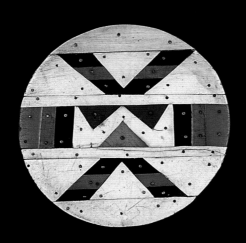

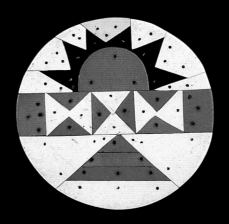

Asia

The mysterious East has fascinated the European imagination for millennia: Ali Baba, and Aladdin were always deeply mysterious figures. Legendary cities with gardens planted with golden trees, bearing fruit in the form of precious stones, together with enchantingly scented princesses, scantily clad in silks and covered with fabulous jewellery, have long haunted the Western mind, and the account of the sixteenth-century Portuguese travellers kept the myth alive.

The Arabian peninsula.

Traditionally, silver has been the preferred material in this region, though gold, formerly used sparingly in Sharqiyah and at Sur, is now tending to replace it. The ear pendants of the region are characterised by the diversity and quality of their chains. Chains with rectangular mesh, doubled into U-shape and narrowing towards the top (pp. 72-73), seem to have been known some three thousand years B.C. among the Egyptian and Sumerian civilizations, from which their use spread to the Near East and the Mediterranean basin[1].

Bedouin women take pride in the weight of their ornaments, because it is an indication of their value. For this reason, certain types of ear ornaments are actually fixed not to the ear itself, but hung from the *mishill*, a headband made of silver chains.

In northern Oman, children wear simple *hilak al udn* hoops until they marry; women too poor to afford the more elaborate styles also make do with this type of hoop in their adult life[2]. Married women wear the *hilak* with a thick hoop encased in wire over a third, and an ovoid bead soldered to one end, sometimes with a pendant and chains (p. 72). Pear-shaped pendants consisting of two cones, soldered at the base, with a hook for hanging them, may take a number of different forms (p. 79).

The jewel collection of a well-off woman will include earrings in the arc of a circle, *nisa* (p. 75), whose ornamental part consists of a truncated cone in silver wire and filigree. The richer among them wear five or six pairs, fixed to a headband, or *mishill*. Such ornaments are worn by Bedouin women who have ceased to be nomadic as a result of the profitable sale of the dates from their palm groves, or a brisk trade in selling fish. Since they are close to their nomadic sisters, these latter may borrow them[3].

In central Oman, young girls fix their hoops into the rims of their ears, while married women suspend them from the lobe. Boys wear a simple hoop in the outer ear, to ward off spirits.

Central Asia

Although it has always been hemmed in by high mountains, the vast steppes of central Asia have never been totally inward-looking. Travellers have visited their oases and caravanserais since antiquity, and centres of trade as well as craftsmanship, are found throughout the region. The cities of Bukhara, Khiva and Samarkand were a melting-pot for mutual influences, where styles and fashions came and went. Afghanistan was a crossroads for the routes linking Iran, China and India, at whose gates Alexander the Great had halted.

Perpetually threatened by natural calamities, subject to the harshest of living conditions linked to the continental climate, the tribes who lived in these regions surrounded themselves with protective charms and talismans. Infant mortality was very high and earrings were put on little girls a few days after birth, to ward off the evil eye. When an Uzbek family finally manages to produce a long-awaited child, fragments of silver are collected from the mothers of seven large families and taken to a goldsmith to make earrings which the child will wear until his marriage[4].

Because of this concern with protecting the head, young girls and brides pay a great deal of attention to earrings, whose shapes and sizes vary according to the wearer's status. Those worn by little girls are small and very simple; those worn by the noblewomen of the khanate of Khiva are quite spectacular, with pendants reaching their shoulders and blending into their neck-laces (p. 92). Nomad women wear ear pendants in the shape of a small dome, known as *ui zirak* because of their resemblance to their felt tents.

Although they have long since converted to Islam, the ethnic groups in question make use of a pre-Islamic iconographical repertoire, reflecting ancient beliefs such as animism, shamanism, totemism and ancestor worship. Uzbek craftsmen have been drawn to the representation of birds since time immemorial, and Kazakhs and Kirghiz honour eagles and falcons as symbols of the sun[5]. The heavenly bodies, such as the moon, are regarded as having life-giving powers, as suggested by the temple ornaments known as *mokhi tillo* (p. 93), and the earrings worn by the Uzbek women of Khorezm. Much used by local craftsmen, as in the sumptuous ear pendants of Bukhara (p. 87), the pearls, whose lustre recalls the light of the moon rising from the sea, are believed to ensure abundant offspring.

The father of the bride-to-be devotes most of the matrimonial settlement to the purchase of jewels, which will remain his daughter's property: as an Uzbek proverb has it, "as long as there are female customers, jewellers will never lack for work."[6]

At their weddings, the women of the oases and steppes are resplendent in their entire panoply of jewellery, which they continue to wear until the birth of their first child; thereafter they adorn themselves only at festive gatherings, gradually abandoning their jewellery and ultimately wearing only rings and a pair of modest earrings when they are past child-bearing age. On coming under her husband's roof, the young Karakalpak bride offers rings and earrings to the adolescent girls and young women of the community.

The names of certain nineteenth-century Kirghiz goldsmiths have come down to us, including those of several women[7]. Bukhara, Khiva, Tashkent and Samarkand were important centres of jewellery-making.

The Indian Sub-Continent

For Indians, sound has long had great symbolic importance, since it lies at the origin of the entire cosmos. "If the Word [...] produced the universe, it did so through the effect of the rhythmic vibration of primordial sound."[8] Emerging from the waves, the conch shell gave life to sound, and the aural cavity, by which sound is apprehended, took on the name of *concha*. Closely linked to the magic of words, the ear required protection against the forces of evil, and ornaments provided it.

The oldest earrings from Asia date from six thousand years before Christ. They were discovered at Mehrgarh, in Pakistan, the probable cradle of the Hindu civilization. Excavations of the cities of Harappa and Mohenjo-Daro brought to light numerous ear discs and cylinders, as well as statuettes of mother goddesses wearing voluminous earrings. Frescoes and sculptures, both Buddhist and Hindu, include figures adorned with complex ornaments. In his study of the subject, Michel Postel has shown that five or six main types of earrings are consistently found from the times of the Maurya and Gupta to the medieval period, and indeed up until today among tribes which have settled in remote places. The tradition of cremation among these peoples explains the absence of necropolises and the ensuing loss of this form of jewelry, making research into the topic even more valuable.

Disc-shaped ornaments, symbolic of the sun, and circular hoops, decorated with concentric circles, solar motifs and flowers, are very widely found. Also included are cylinders and mushroom-shaped ornaments. Earrings in the shape of a crescent moon are also known, proving that this motif predates Islamic times. The ear lobe was gradually stretched by cylinders and discs formed of a band of metal[9], such so-called *sisapatras* being the metal version of a rolled up palm leaf, still worn in Bihar and Indonesia. Shell earplugs, in shankha (*Xancus pyrum*), serve propitiatory purposes, because they originate in the ocean and, due to their internal spiral, remind the human inner ear.

Indian earrings range from the most modest, made of alloys of mediocre quality, to the most sumptuous, worn exclusively by the élite, since large and heavy gold pendants were a royal prerogative. Even the tribal peoples wear ornaments in precious metals. Earrings are heightened with encrustation of stones, or glass substitutes. The Rabari of Kutch wear several pairs of gold or silver pairs at once (p. 143).

Golds jewels represent much more than a mere accumulation of precious goods, as proved by the very ancient symbolism associated with them, though its meaning is often obscure. One of the legends concerning the origin of gold in India tells how Agni, the god of fire, in a state of intense arousal, turned his gaze upon earth's waters, and finally poured his seed upon them, causing it to metamorphose into little glittering pearls; gold has been found in rivers ever since[10].

The women of South India have a passion for gold, using it in their ear lobes, rims and outer ears. Among Hindu, the tradition of wearing such ornaments has persisted almost unchanged over the ages, since men and women alike continue to believe that it protects them from evil spirits. Ascetics will renounce everything except for earrings[11].

The Naga, or "naked people" of East Assam, a Mongolian people who seem to have migrated from northern China several millennia ago, have remained animist, regarding the head as the seat of the essential being, and assiduously practising head hunting in order to increase their vital energy.

Apart from expressing aesthetic preferences, jewels also serve to differentiate between the tribes, and to indicate the individual's status within them. Some of the various types of ear ornaments may be worn by all alike, while others are the privilege of one social category, or indeed of one specific person. The Angami wear the hair of the slain enemy in their ears, in order to appropriate

his vital force. Young Ao girls adorn themselves with red pimentos.

The Ao father pierces his child's ears the second day after birth. At the age of three months, Ao boys are given an ornament in goat's hair which they remove only when they are admitted into the *morung*, where unmarried boys go to be initiated into the customs and beliefs of the tribe[12]. The iridescent feathers of the Indian roller, or blue jay, are particularly appreciated by Ao men, who ornament their lobes with the whole wing[13]. At seedtime, among the Lotha, a sterile old woman goes to the fields and makes an offering, while at weddings the same woman lays a leaf on the couple's ears, thus establishing a link between seedtime – the root of all fertility – and marriage, the prerequisite for human fecundity[14].

Among the Konyak, the wearing of ornaments made of *Xancus*, from the distant Indian Ocean, is a male prerogative; such ornaments are decorated with stylised figures – similar to the cowrie shells applied to fabrics – or with a V motif, reminiscent of buffalo horns, which warriors wear tattooed on their chests (p. 149).

The Naga obtain metal – in the form of wire, sheet and ingots – from the plain of Assam or at Manipur, with their preference going to brass. Ao women wear superbly refined ornaments in rock crystal or glass (p. 150).

The Himalayas

Few very old jewels from this region have survived. The ancient tombs of Tibet have been ransacked, and the tradition of keeping family jewels intact died out during the course of the nineteenth century. In Nepal, changes in taste have brought about immense losses. Women nowadays no longer wear large ear ornaments, which they regard as old-fashioned and disfiguring. A considerable rise in population over the last century led to the melting down of bulky old jewels to make up for the lack of available gold. Accounts of European travellers from the end of the eighteenth century are the most reliable source for any knowledge of the older types.

The inhospitable climate of the Himalayas fostered the growth of numerous beliefs, and those who do not have pierced ears, or do not wear earrings, are regarded as in danger of being reincarnated as donkeys. Ear piercing is believed to ward off illness and evil generally, lending credence to the thesis of those anthropologists who maintain that the original function of jewellery was apotropaic rather than ornamental[15].

The tolerant nature of the local inhabitants enables Hinduism and Buddhism to coexist side by side, with hints of animist and shamanist substrata. The Gods are depicted as lavishly bedecked with jewellery, including large ear ornaments, as we see on a small terracotta from Lumbini dating from the third millennium B.C.

The Newar – originally from the valley of Katmandu, but who settled in Tibet centuries ago – were renowned goldsmiths, working for the ruling class and aristocracy in their workshops at the foot of the Potala, at Lhasa, as the Chinese of the frontier towns did for the Mongols. Tibetan society, with its strong sense of hierarchy, considered jewellery as an emblem of rank and wealth. Old photographs show dignitaries and their wives proudly decked out in their various ornaments, including sumptuous earrings in gold and turquoise mosaic (p. 160). Worn one beside the other, they were attached to the headdress to avoid the lobes being torn. Squabbling women are said to grab each other by the ear lobe[16]. Men ornament their left lobe with an earring, and the right one with a simply pierced, unpolished turquoise.

In Nepal young women wear many ornaments, since jewellery acts as a lure for future husbands. When they are past childbearing age, they hand over some of their parures to younger women[17]. As the purest part of the body, the head is the object of particular attention, and is lavishly adorned with jewels in gold, which is a sacred metal. Gold and turquoise are the two most sought after in the hierarchy of precious materials in Tibet. Further-

more, as we learn from Sangye Gyatso (1653-1705) in his medical treatise The Blue Beryl, gold has healing properties and prolongs life, while turquoise protects against poisons and diseases of the liver[18].

The best-known ear ornaments from Nepal are the *cheptisun* (p. 153) and the *dhungri*. *Cheptisun* are large discs, composed of an extremely thin sheet of gold, with a split in their upper rim for insertion into the ear lobe; the structure of the ring, which may be as much as ten centimetres in diameter, is reinforced by the superimposition of a central band, decorated with stylised floral motifs. *Repoussé Dhungri*, which may be both round and square (p. 152), are worn in the outer ear, and are reminiscent of earrings from Rajasthan; indeed, from the twelfth to fourteenth centuries the Rajput, a warrior caste from Rajasthan, took refuge in the kingdom of Khas on their flight from the Muslim invaders. Local jewellery might have been influenced by the ornaments which married women brought back from India in their dowries, and by the fact that various goldsmiths probably followed them.

China

In China, too, long ears are a sign of wisdom and immortality. The ears of Laozi, known as "long ears", were seven inches long[19]. Excavations in tombs of the Ming period (1368-1644) have brought to light a number of earrings (pp. 166-167) reflecting an age-old tradition of highly sophisticated craftsmanship.

Over the centuries the Han attempted to dominate the other national minorities, whom they regarded as "primitive barbarians"; the central authorities always encouraged Han migration towards the West and South-West of the country in the hope of keeping them under control. However, when the jewels made by these supposedly inferior minorities were at last discovered by European travellers, they aroused surprise and enthusiasm for the beauty and diversity of their forms, often extremely modern, and the quality of the craftsmanship.

One of the main minorities, the Miao, can boast of a very ancient culture, their ancestors having moved southwards from the Hunang basin over the millennia to settle mainly in Hunan, Guizhou and Yunnan. Despite harsh living conditions in inhospitable terrain, the Miao have a strongly developed sense of occasion; they are particularly noted for their love songs, sung in alternating duets by young men and women during dances to the sound of the *lusheng*, a sort of mouth-organ. Every village has a meadow, or public garden, set aside for these poetry contests, where love affairs often blossom.

Decked out in their finery, woven and embroidered by their own hand, and wearing their sumptuous ornaments, the girls are exquisitely graceful. Their almost sculptural hairstyles and headdresses are breathtakingly beautiful, and include an endless variety of chignons and turbans; hair pieces combined with wool, pins, combs and earrings make them genuine works of art. Their dowries take the form of jewels, which are both things of beauty and a sign of wealth.

When a young man becomes engaged, his parents choose a favourable moment, some days before the wedding, to pay a visit to the village of the bride-to-be, taking with them engagement presents in the form of handmade fabrics and silver jewellery, including earrings.

The girls of eastern Guizhou are lavish in their use of jewellery as ornaments are a symbol of light and they drive off demons and ensure safety[20]; almost every village has an expert goldsmith. Very varied in form, earrings may be cast, or made out of worked wire, often with a pendant with a floral motif, enamelled or otherwise. Cascades of filigree and little chains also figure, together with hoops of all sizes, sometimes decorated with discs of jade, particularly prized by the Chinese. Like the Meo of the Golden Triangle, the Miao form one immense family with countless branches, which has become dispersed over the course of the centuries, so that it should come as no surprise that we find the same type of earrings among the Dong (cf. p. 189), who live in the same provinces, as well as beyond the Chinese frontiers.

Mongolia

In Mongolia, little girls have their ears pierced at an early age, in order to be ready for the day when some small boy, aged about seven, will bring them a pair of silver earrings, acceptance of which implies tacit agreement to a subsequent betrothal[21]. Earrings and headdress pendants, bracelets, rings and headdresses themselves, together with camels, horses and cattle, make up the matrimonial settlement offered by the suitor's family to that of the bride. Among the Ordos, earrings are one of the "five white gifts" presented during the wedding ceremony[22]. In Western Mongolia, custom requires that women wear earrings in pairs, while young girls wear them singly, as do men[23]. Among the Torgut of Tian Shan, the young men who wear a single earring in their left ear will have offered the other to their bride-to-be[24].

Several types of Mongolian earrings may strike us as familiar, the Mongols borrowed indeed extensively from the Tibetans, not only in terms of their choice of material but also in terms of models and techniques, and in their way of wearing them. Because of their excessive weight, most earrings, or *süike*, cannot be worn in the ear lobe, but are fixed to a band running over the head, to the headdress, or to some other ornament. Most probably in earlier times large hoops hung around the ear adapting itself to the shape[25] (p. 206).

Craftsmen borrow their themes from Chinese iconography and from Buddhism, whose teachings were taught them by the Tibetans.

South-East Asia

The vast area stretching between Vietnam and Burma has been home to a number of kingdoms and various great centres of civilization. Although influenced by their Indian and Chinese neighbours, the Pyu in Burma, the Khmer in Cambodia and the Cham in Vietnam elaborated a style of their own, in which Hinduism and Buddhism, mingled with animist concepts, were grafted on to the Dongson legacy. Motifs such as the double spiral, typical of this Bronze Age culture, have survived until the present day in isolated areas.

The oldest earrings are in shell and stone (pp. 216-217): being very hard materials, they protect the living and accompany the dead on their journey to their new life. At first very simple in form, these ornaments became more complex with the discovery of the various metals, and as techniques progressed. Extraordinarily inventive variations on the theme of the split hoop continued to be devised from the neolithic period right down to the twentieth century. Trade and migration contributed to its diffusion, but its enduring popularity can really only be explained by its symbolic association.

The Pyu, originally from China, dominated Burma during the first millennium, and contemporary Chinese writings express amazement at the sumptuousness of life at the court of Sri-ksetra: gold cylinders, with the finest filigree work, and mounted rubies (p. 211), bear witness to this refinement. The Pyu are regarded as great lovers of gemstones. The influence of the Indian courts is visible in the frescoes at Pagan (1044-1287), where queens are seen wearing huge ear discs.

The minority groups produce a great variety of ear ornaments. In the North, Kachin women wear long cylinders of amber, while the Shan wear equivalents in jade. Karen women wear bands of rolled metal, or imitations in the form of a large disc, with a dominant spiral motif. The Karen also make exceptional ornaments in honey or amber coloured ivory, like little pestles, with handles of varying lengths, sometimes of extraordinary thinness (pp. 238-239). The Bre use bobbins as ornaments (pp. 236-237).

The Akha, Lisu and Lahu, who speak Tibeto-Burmese languages, left China in the eighteenth and nineteenth centuries to settle in the inhospitable regions of the Golden Triangle, in Eastern Burma, Thailand and Northern Laos. The constant migrations of large groups of people make it difficult to attribute a precise geographical origin to any one type of earring, since the same type may be found in areas quite remote the one from the other.

The Hmong, known as Meo in Thailand and as Miao in China, are very fond of silver ornaments, and wear a large range of earrings expressing their particular love of clean forms. The most striking are the long stem-like ornaments ending in a button-shaped motif (p. 218), while the most attractive are the mini-torques, and the rings flat in section, superbly engraved with geometrical motifs, with and without a pendant (pp. 228-232). Surprisingly enough, the ornaments of two of these peoples – the Meo and Miao – include very few types of finger rings.

The Cham are believed to be the descendants of the Sa Huynh of the coastal regions of Vietnam, who then migrated from the Indian archipelago towards the mainland[26]. The wealth of the kingdom of Champa was based on lumber, and intense maritime trade. Split earrings in glass, semi-precious stones, gold and gilded sheet silver have there been found (pp. 210-211).

Moulds discovered at Oc Eo, in the ancient Indianised kingdom of Funan, reveal models similar to those found in Java at the same period. Close links, through marriage or diplomatic relations, were forged between Champa, Cambodia and Java[27]. The Khmer invaded Champa, but the Cham regained the upper hand in 1177. From the eleventh century onwards, contact with Muslim traders led to many conversions to Islam and hence to access to a new iconographical and stylistic repertoire.

The Indian Archipelago

The Philippines were on the route taken by the migrants who, driven by pressure from a rising population, left Southern China thousands of years ago and crossed the seas on outrigger boats; some then left the Philippines in their turn for the Indian and Melanesian archipelagoes. Ear discs in shell, which might date back five thousand years, have been discovered by archaeologists in tombs at Palawan[28]. We also know of glass ornaments (dating from 200 B.C. - 100 A.D.) very similar to the stone ornaments of Vietnam, and other split ornaments, which prove how far trade in such items must date back.

Of the thousands of islands in the Philippine archipelago, two are of particular interest for our purposes: Mindanao, to the south, and Luzon, to the north. Islamized from the fourteenth century, Mindanao, whose inhabitants had sustained relations with those of Sulawesi, Borneo and the Malaysian peninsula, were never conquered by the Spanish.

Bagobo women wear elegant ear pendants in mother-of-pearl, hung from copper chains and sometimes from bone buttons. Men wear *pamarang* exquisitely shaped and patinated earplugs in ivory (pp. 245 and 247).

The north of Luzon, whose gold and copper were much coveted by the Spanish conquistadors, was never in fact conquered by them, though the culture of the *Igorot*, or mountain-dwellers, was influenced by their presence over a period of three centuries. Gold jewels, including "earrings of fine gold" mentioned by Miranda in 1594[29], were found in abundance in the Cordillera. Sadly, they were seized and melted down by the Spaniards without having been described.

The most interesting items from the period which concerns us here are split earrings, which have antecedents dating back to prehistory but which have constantly taken on new forms as metaphors for fecundity. The basic form is an almost completely closed C-shape, the more elaborate being zoomorphic and anthropomorphic (p. 250); they may be made of gold, silver or brass, according to the wearer's means, and are common to several ethnic groups.

The Kalinga attach great importance to antique items, as Barton tells us: "Their gold earrings, whose intrinsic value ranges from 20–40 pesos, may be worth four or five times this sum if they are old."[30]

Extremely sophisticated and meticulous craftsmen, the *Ilongot* make exquisite little mother-of-pearl earrings (p. 251). A successful headhunting expedition earns a man the right to wear the *batling*, made of the red beak of the hornbill, decorated with delicate little mother-of-pearl elements which catch the light (p. 249). Celebrated in songs and speeches, his prowess earns him the respect of the young women.

The ancient Indonesian island societies were part of the great current of Megalithic cultures, with their predominantly animist outlook. The influence of Tonkin and Cochinchina was decisive as far as jewellery was concerned, as we see from examples from the first centuries of the modern era. A flourishing agriculture produced surpluses which made it possible to support craftsmen and to develop extremely complex ritual systems based on barter. Indonesia's natural riches caused it to become a port of call on the sea route linking India and China. Indeed, the burgeoning of the brilliant Hindu-Javanese culture of the so-called classical period was made possible by a knowledge of Indian religious ideas, and of India's advanced technical achievements.

Contrary to legend, Java does not seem to have had much gold of its own, and probably obtained its supplies from Sumatra and Borneo[31]. The earrings from central Java dating from the ancient classical period (700-1000), are characterised by their simplicity of form, with the exception of two types, namely the ornaments reminiscent of clouds or mountains, such as mount Meru, symbols of the spiritual purification practised by ascetics in high and lonely places, believed to be the abode of their ancestors (p. 257), and the small baroque ornaments, often called bird rings, which represent the *vajra*, an attribute of the Hindu god Indra (p. 256).

More sophisticated techniques, such as chasing,

made possible the creation of more complex motifs in the recent classical period, which had its apogee in the eastern part of the island under the Majapahit empire (1293-1528). Both the iconographical repertoire and the techniques used remained unaffected by the penetration of Islamic ideas until after 1500.

Situated on the trade route leading to South-East Asia, and on the spice route of Estern Indonesia, Sumatra had an extraordinarily cosmopolitan history. A prosperous Chinese community developed a court culture there in the fifteenth century. In the sixteenth, various Islamic traders, fleeing the Portuguese presence on the Malaysian peninsula, laid siege to the sultanate of Aceh and went on to develop techniques for the making of filigree and granulation, as exemplified by the studs on page 263. The ruling class also enjoyed close relations with the Ottoman empire under Suleiman the Magnificent[32].

The Minangkabau who had settled around Padang, on the west coast, had access to its goldmines, and engaged in international trade. Under the influence of Aceh, they adopted new techniques, as we see from their magnificent gold studs (pp. 264-265). Their renowned goldsmiths travelled from village to village, and their repertoire was enriched accordingly. The Karo Batak benefitted from their expertise. The very delicately worked silver-gilt ear pendants shown on page 261, are worn during *adat* festivals, but only by the ruling class. Formerly worn in pairs by women of all ages, the impressive double spiral *padung-padung* show the influence of the archaic ornamental tradition (p. 266).

In the past, the casting and working of gold – spiritually meaningful activities which were regarded as dangerous – required the taking of various precautionary measures; before setting to work, the goldsmith proceeded to prayers and propitiatory sacrifices, as indeed was customary in most societies.

The Toba Batak, who have lived a more isolated existence, are known for their spectacular bronze ornaments. The men wear the asymmetrical *sitepal* in their left ear

lobe, and the symmetrical *duri duri* in their left (p. 259). Their shape may be interpreted in various ways: as a local variant of the stylised *naga* or womb, according to Anne Richter[33], or as a mythical creature coiled up around itself, like an insect, according to Susan Rodgers[34].

The entire social organization of the Batak is structured around an asymmetrical system of alliances between the givers and takers of wives, and the rituals accompanying such exchanges have enormous symbolic significance. The givers of wives make gifts of fabrics whose softness embodies the female element; in exchange, they receive objects in metal, including earrings, which are associated with the masculine element. Like jewels, speeches and dances, textiles too – an essential component of costume – convey concepts and have mythical undertones.

The highly stratified society of the island of Nias is made up of the aristocracy, the common people, and slaves. Intensely aware of their superiority, the nobility enjoy privileged relations with the supernatural world and organise large parties to enhance their prestige, during which they make great show of ornaments in gold – a noble metal – such as earrings consisting of a sheet of metal forming a double scroll (p. 269).

Borneo has a long and proud history of involvement in international trade, having supplied South-East Asia with diamonds – *intan* – since at least the fifteenth century. The island now consists of one Malaysian province, Sarawak, and one Indonesian one, Kalimantan. The name Dayak, meaning people of the uplands or interior, covers several tribes: the Apo Kayan, the Kenyah of Kalimantan and the Iban of Sarawak. They have close cultural links with the tribes of Mindanao, of the interior of the island of Luzon, and of the interior of Sulawesi, and are animist societies which practise headhunting. Extremely distended ear lobes are their ideal of beauty; lobes are stretched to the desired length with metal hoops whose weight and number gradually increase over time. Torn lobes are a source of shame for the Dayak, since they cannot be used as supports for displays of prestigious ornaments.

The Kenyah and Kayan wear large brass hoops, cast with the lost wax process (p. 273), ending in the head of an *aso* dragon, a female underworld goddess of fertility. The same motif is found on fabrics, *tapa*, tattoos and sculpture. Heine-Geldern regarded this curvilinear style as a borrowing from the Chinese art of the end of the Chou period[35]. Ornaments carved from the beak of the hornbill, regarded as a mythical bird in South-East Asia, are worn only by men who have been successful in headhunting. Warriors of noble rank wear large ornaments whose base is decorated with the *aso* motif set in openwork tracery (p. 271). The use of the casque of the hornbill enables craftsmen to put its typical alternating red and yellow colouring to highly inventive effect.

The Sunda Islands are regularly visited by travelling goldsmiths from the small island of Ndao, who leave it in the dry season to work for the local families; this sometimes makes it difficult to attribute an exact place of origin to any given jewel, since the types found are often very similar.

Gold earrings are worn by local chiefs and are a sign of wealth; they are part of the family treasure, but may also play a part in matrimonial exchanges. Similarly shaped earrings in silver are worn by the ordinary people. *Wea*, inserted into the distended earlobes of the Lio of Flores, are part of the collection of precious objects which the woman takes with her to her husband. Gold earrings – *wea wunu wona* (p. 281) – act as an advance payment of the dowry. The Ngada living in the center of the island, display the motif of the *bela* (p. 283) on the high-reliefs of their houses.

Thanks to a long history of trade with the Javanese and then with the Portuguese, the inhabitants of Timor were able to accumulate riches which enabled them to purchase a great deal of jewellery, particularly in silver. Although several ethnic groups have never mastered the goldsmith's art, they nonetheless have a wide range of ornaments at their disposal, particularly earrings and bracelets.

As a result of their trading activities with the Dutch colonizer, in both slaves and horses, the aristocracy of Sumba became immensely wealthy; in the past only the *rajas* and their families were allowed to own gold jewellery. The best-known type of local earring is that of the *mamuli*, a large split ornament (p. 290). In eastern Sumba, simple versions were originally worn only by women, and later occasionally by men, who then gradually appropriated them for their own exclusive use. This jewel can be worn in various ways on festive occasions: suspended from a string running around the ear, fixed to a turban or as a pendant. A sign of wealth, it is offered by the *raja* to local chiefs to ensure himself of their loyalty and to proclaim his own power. Embellished with zoomorphic motifs similar to those seen on *ikat* textiles, such ornaments are part of the family heirlooms and kept hidden in the lofts of *adat* houses. As an embodiment of the family's ancestry, they may also facilitate contact with the ancestral spirits, the *marapu*, which explains their value as sacred and inalienable relics.

The wealth of the Moluccas – the last beads in the chaplet of Indonesian islands – was founded on the trade in cloves and nutmeg. The elite particularly prized the gold and elephant ivory which the skilled silversmiths of Makassar procured for them in exchange for copra, shells and tortoiseshell. In their power struggles, the aristocracy engaged in ostentatious contests taking the form of ritualised jousts. Metal-working, linked to the supernatural world, is very highly regarded at Tanimbar, and is the monopoly of a few favoured families.

This journey through the archipelagoes has revealed something of the symbolic implications of the jewel: earrings are illustrative of the fundamental concept according to which the union of complementary elements, by engendering the creative force which ensures issue, serves as a guarantee of the survival of the clan and tribe.

[1] *Dictionnaire du bijou*, p. 118.
[2] Morris, Shelton, *Oman Adorned*, p. 71.
[3] Morris, Shelton, *op.cit.*, p. 75.
[4] Fakhretdinova, *Jeweller's art of Uzbekistan*, p. 174.
[5] Sychova, *Traditional Jewellery from Societ Central Asia*, p. 17.
[6] Fakhretdinova, *op. cit.*, p. 168.
[7] Sychova, *op. cit.*, p. 24.
[8] Chevalier, Gheerbrant, *Dictionnaire des Symboles*, p. 897.
[9] Postel, *Ear ornaments of India*, p. 28.

[10] Weihreter, *Alter Goldschmuck aus Indien*, p. 7.
[11] Weihreter, *op. cit.*, p. 71.
[12] Jacobs *et al.*, *Les Naga*, p. 56.
[13] Untracht, *Traditional Jewelry of India*, p. 60.
[14] Jacobs, *op. cit.*, p. 38.
[15] Gabriel, *Jewelry of Nepal*, p. 14.
[16] MacLeod, quoted by Olson, *Catalogue of the Tibetan collection*, p. 62.
[17] Gabriel, *op. cit.*, p. 19.
[18] Singer, *Gold Jewelry from Tibet and Nepal*, p. 33.

[19] Chevalier, Gheerbrant, *op. cit.*, p. 709.
[20] The Cultural Palace, *Clothing and Ornaments of China's Miao People*, p. 64
[21] Boyer, *Mongol Jewelry*, p. 155.
[22] Boyer, *op. cit.*, p. 155.
[23] Pallas, quoted by Boyer, *op. cit.*, p. 155.
[24] Bonvalot quoted by Boyer, *op. cit.*, p. 155.
[25] Boyer, *op. cit.*, p. 155.
[26] Richter, *The Jewelry of Southeast Asia*, p. 57.

[27] Richter, *op. cit.*, p. 60.
[28] Richter, *op. cit.*, p. 243.
[29] Kising quoted by Ellis, *The People and Art of the Philippines*, p. 242.
[30] Quoted by Rodgers, *L'Or des îles*, p. 243.
[31] Miksic, *Small Finds*, p. 7.
[32] Richter, *op. cit.*, p. 157.
[33] Richer, *op. cit.*, p. 202.
[34] Rodgers, *op. cit.*, p. 321.
[35] Rodgers, *op. cit.*, p. 38 and Richter, *op. cit.*, p. 174.

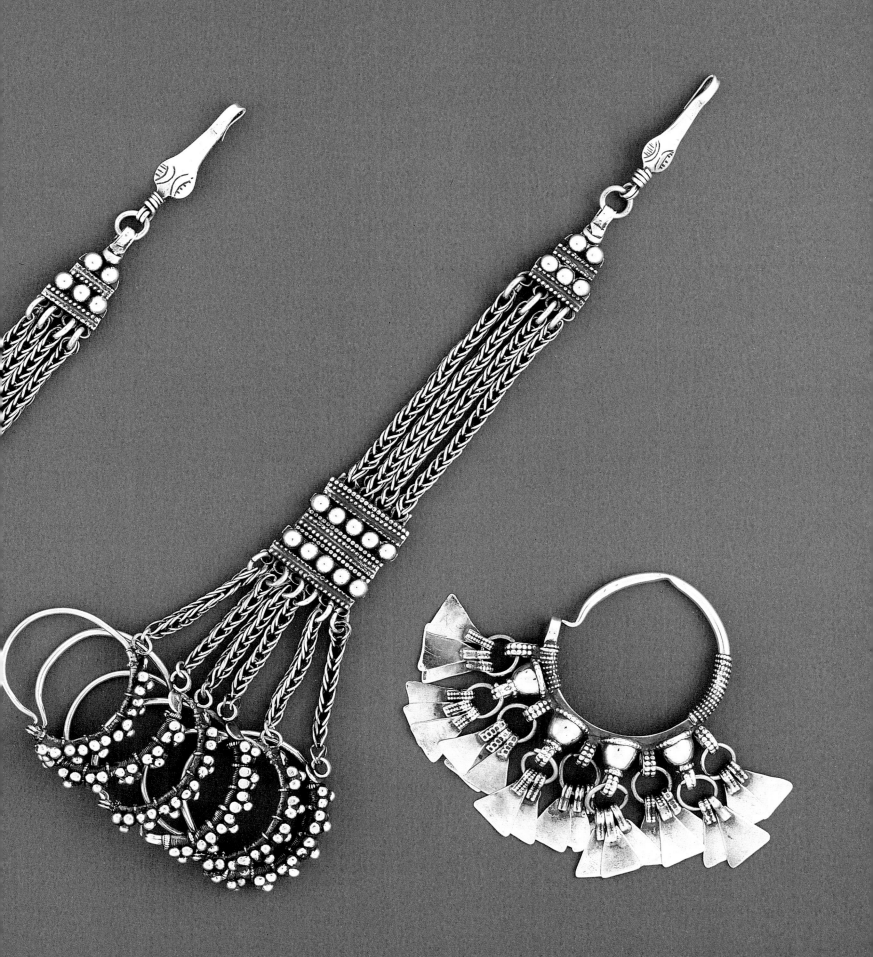

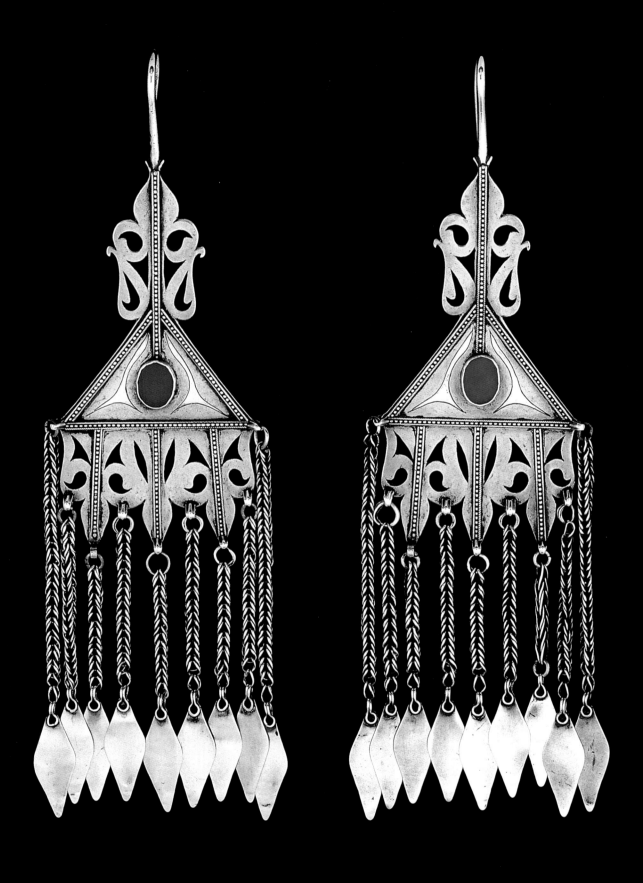

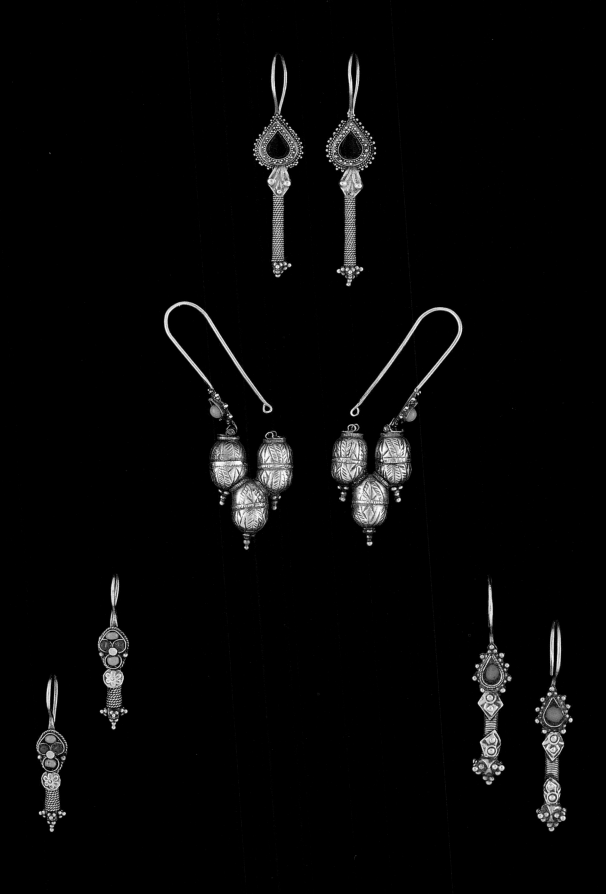

88

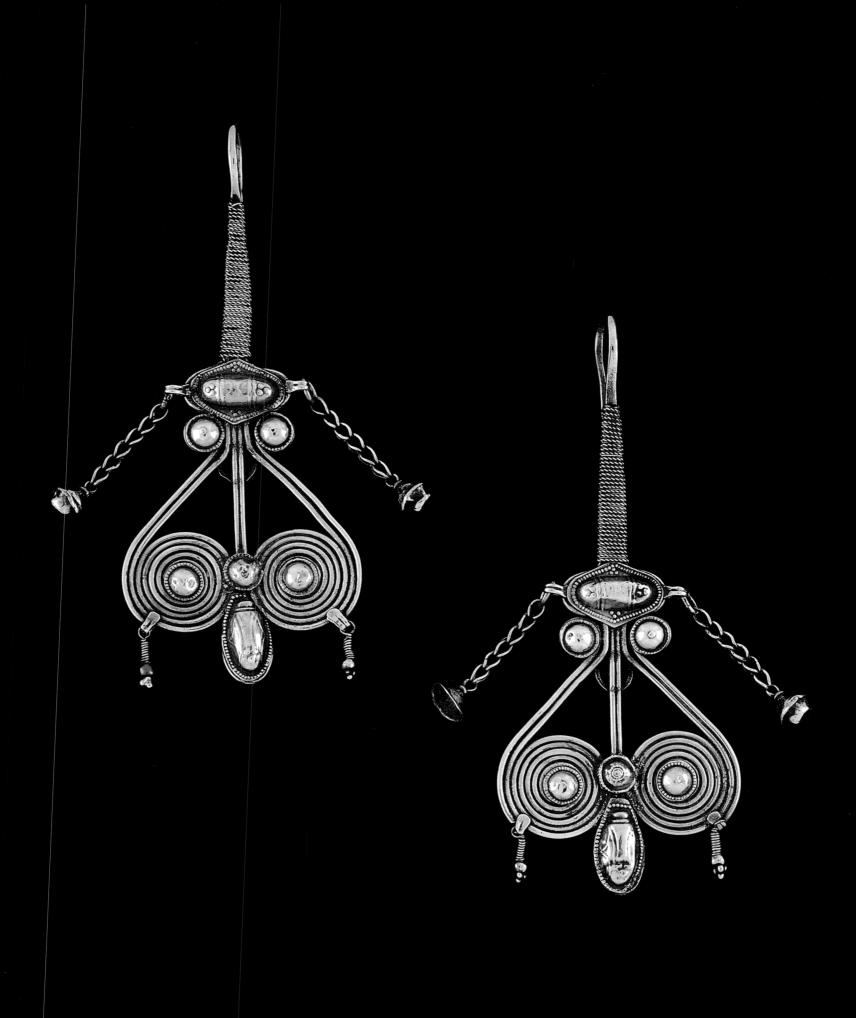

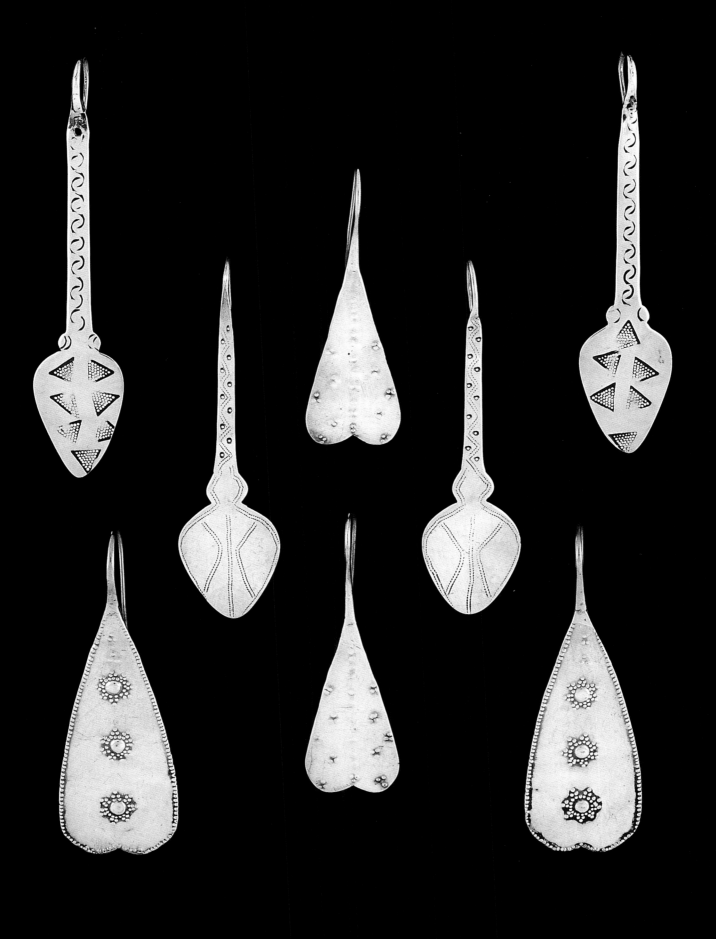

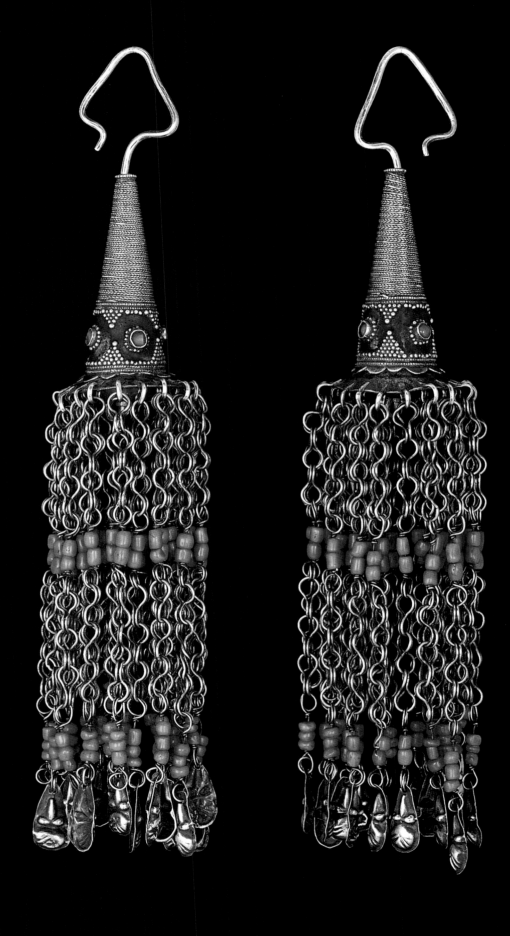

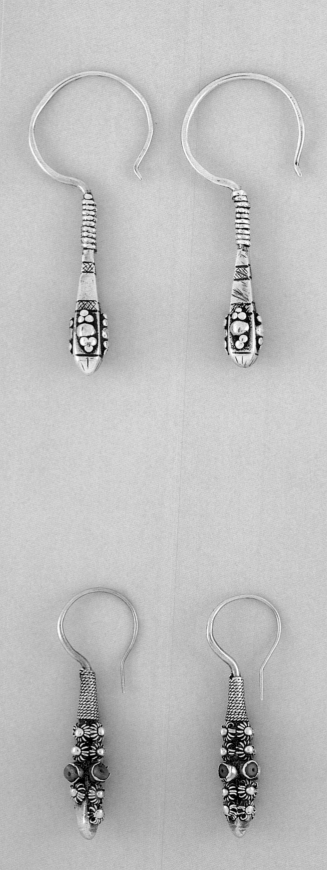

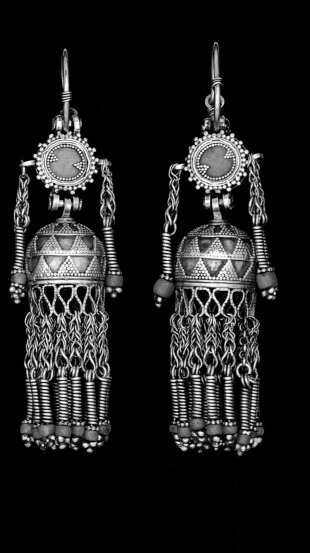

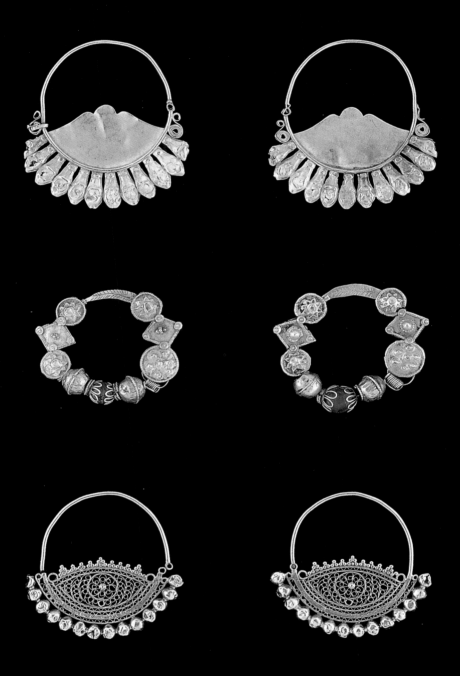

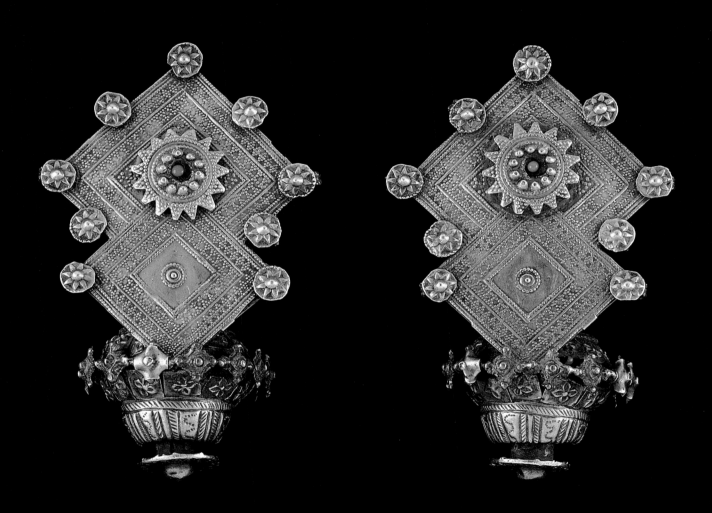

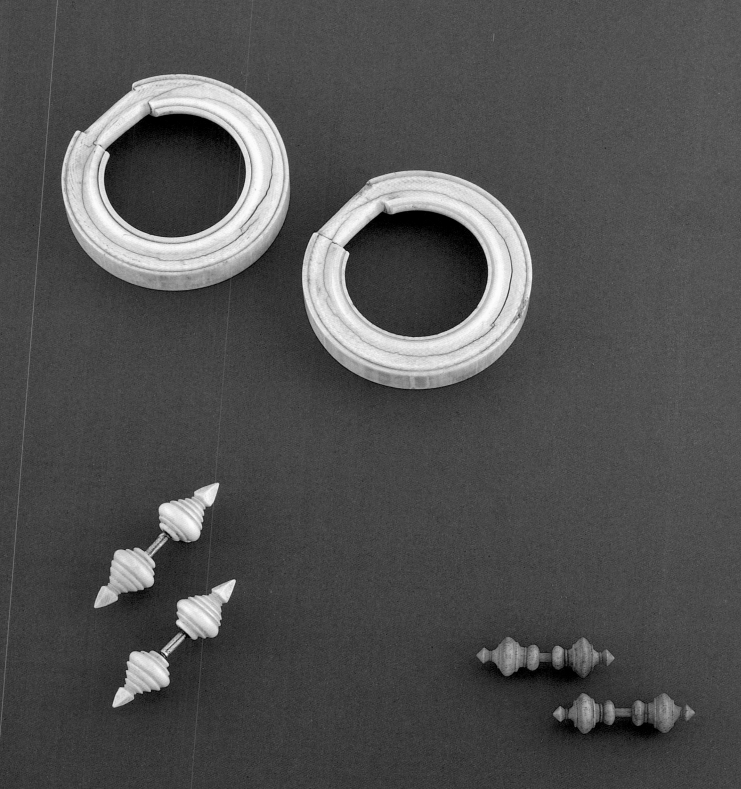

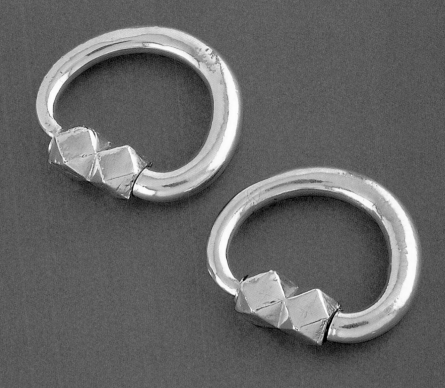

118

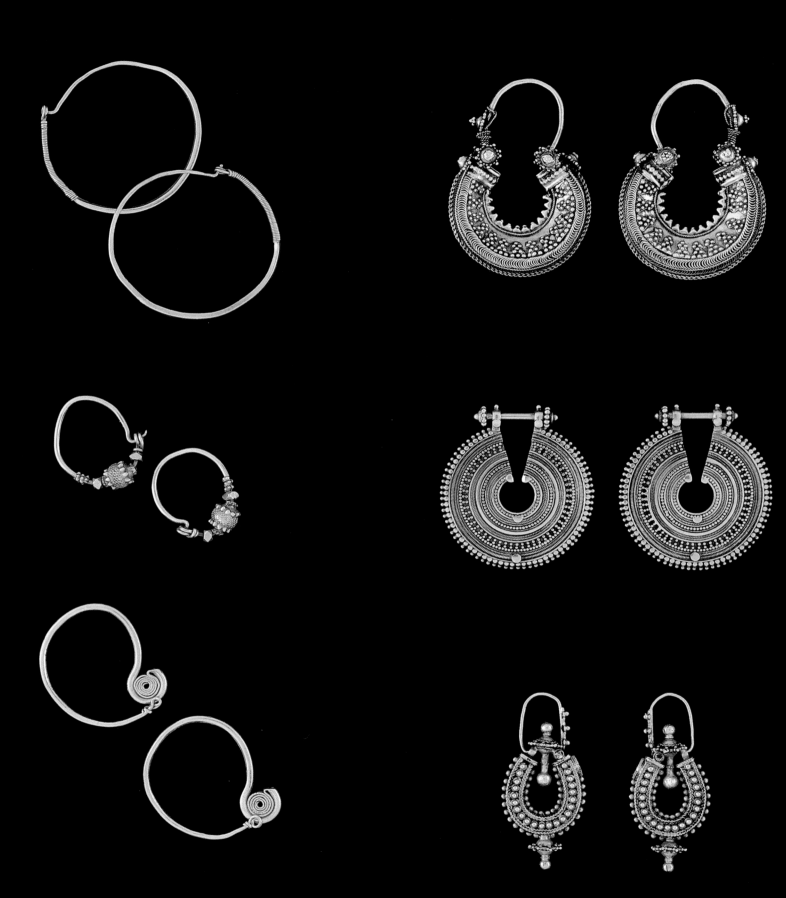

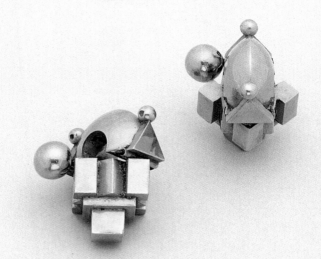

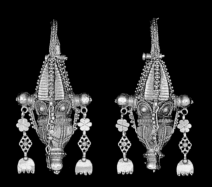

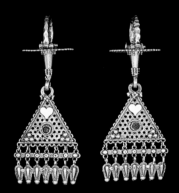

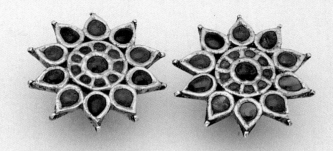

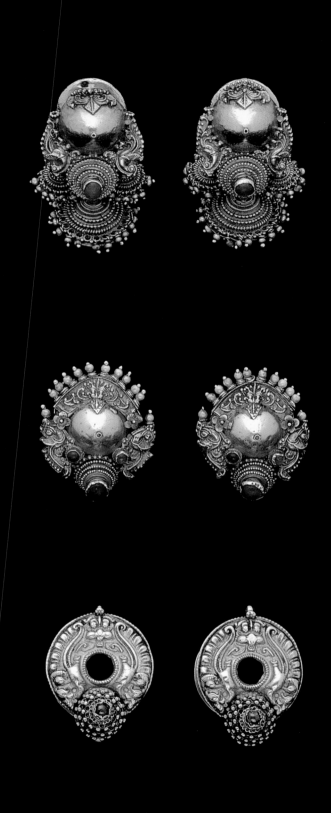

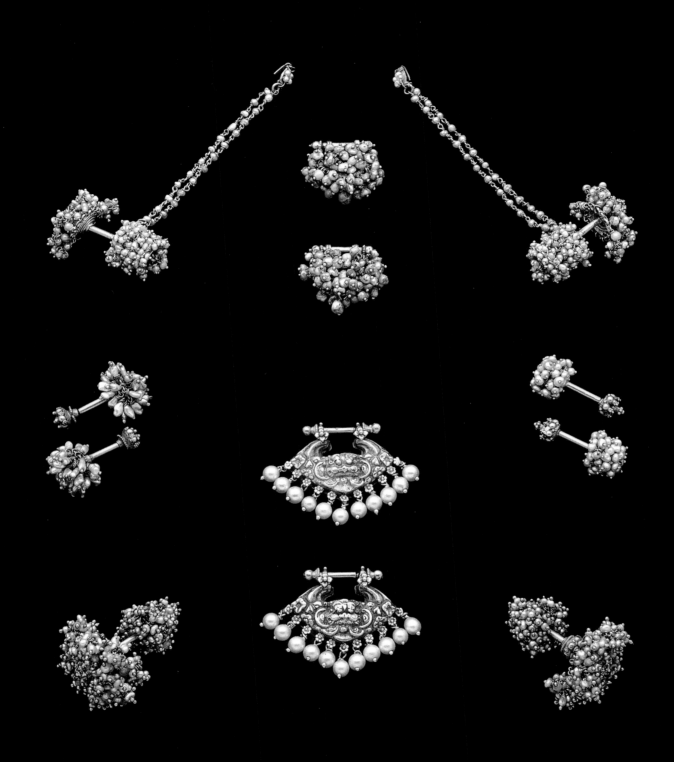

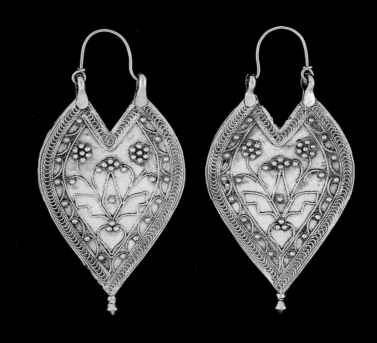

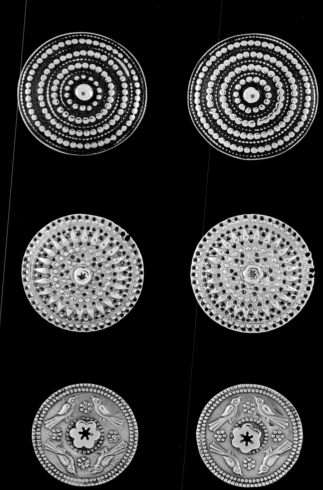

132

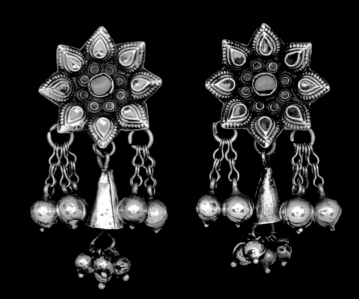
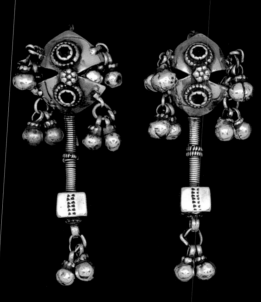

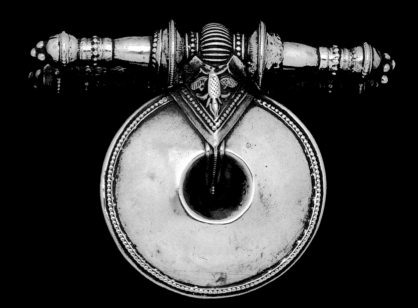
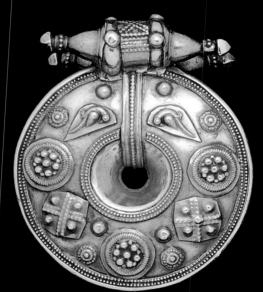

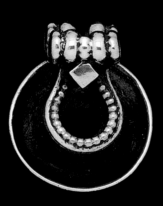

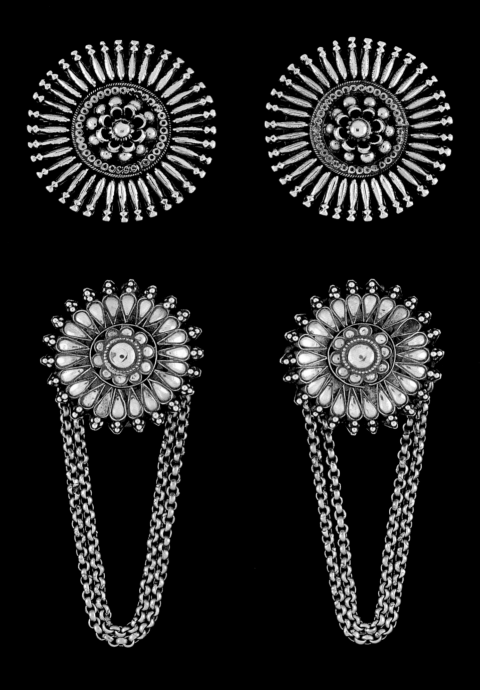

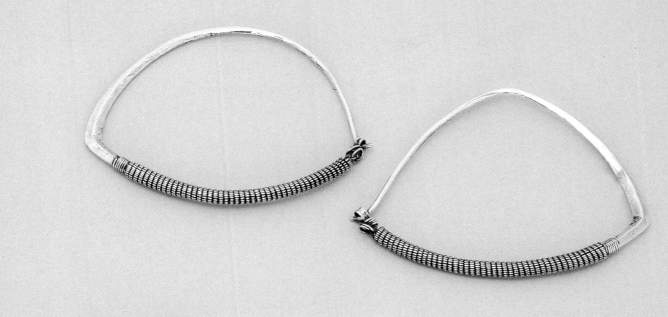

143

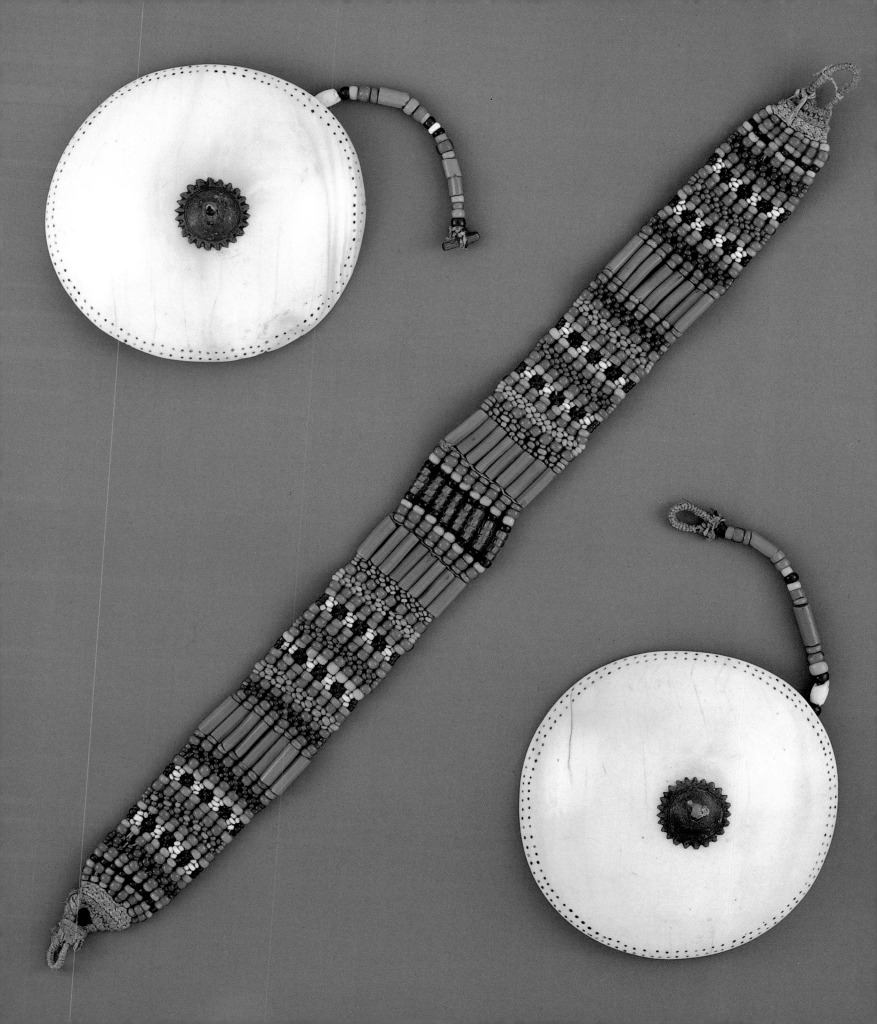

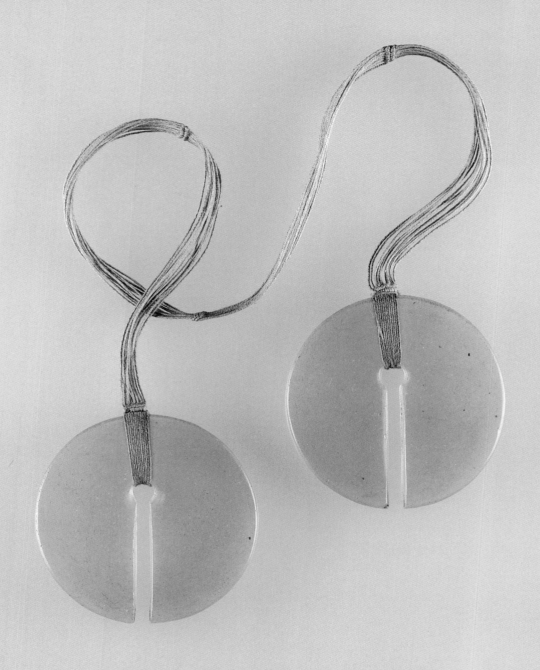

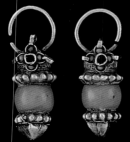

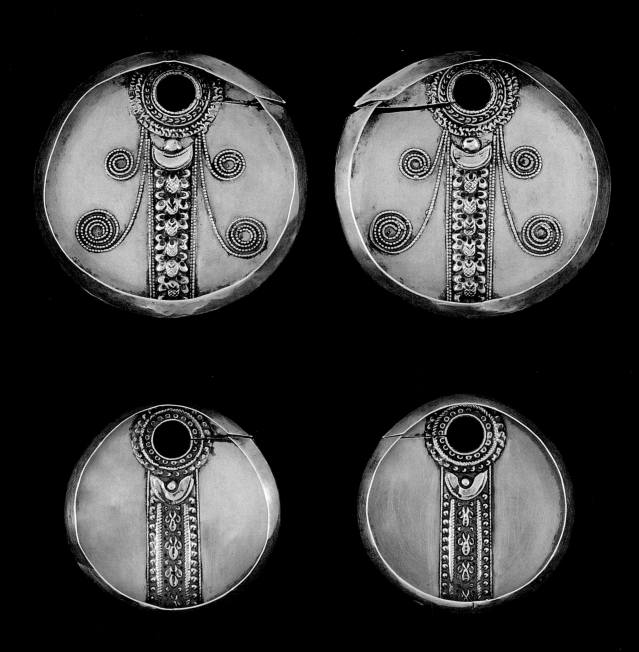

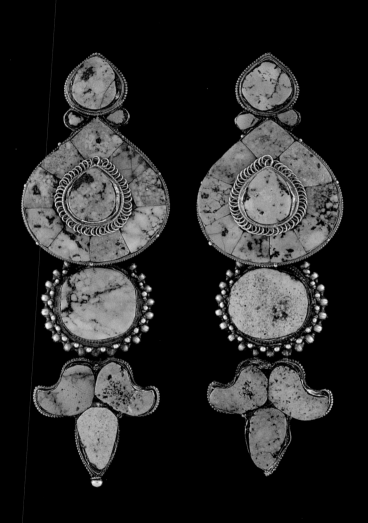

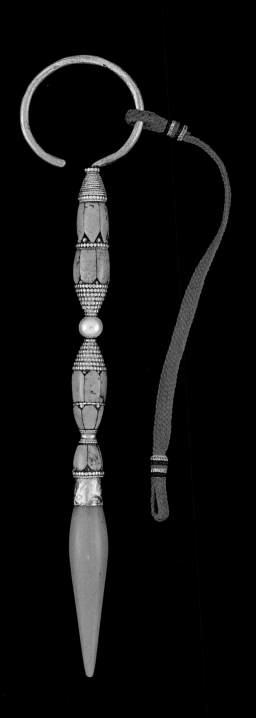

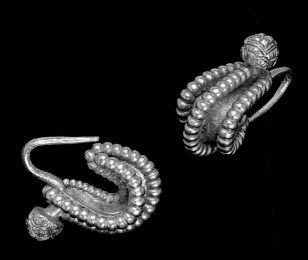

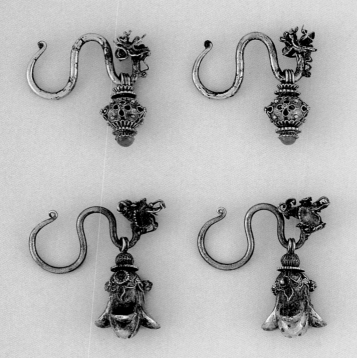

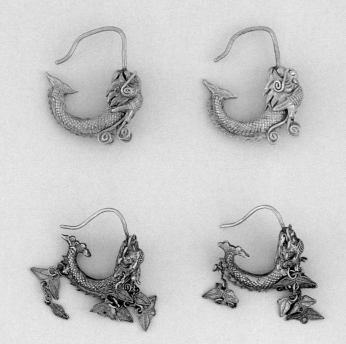

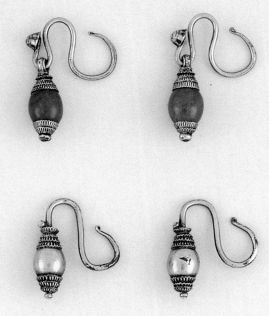

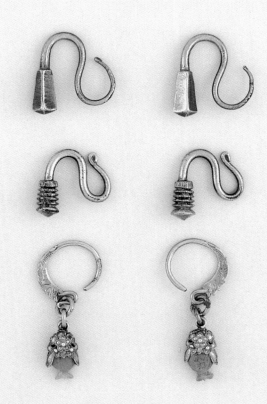

168

169

171

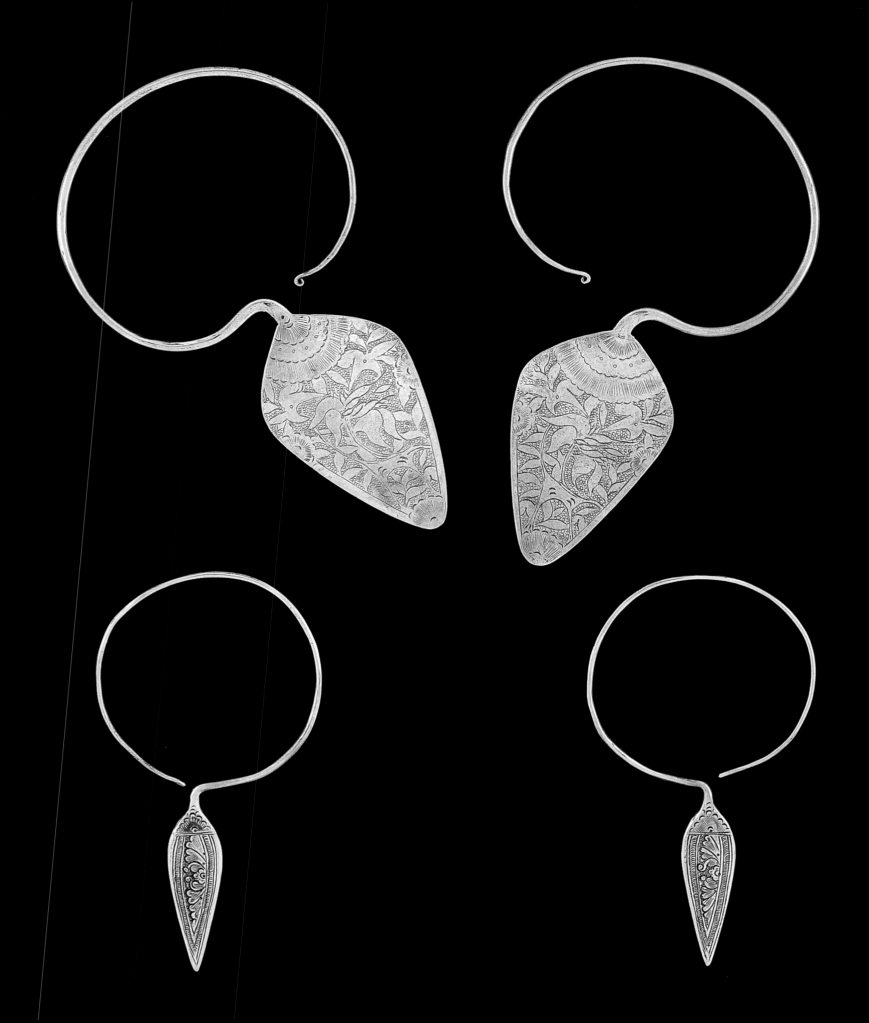

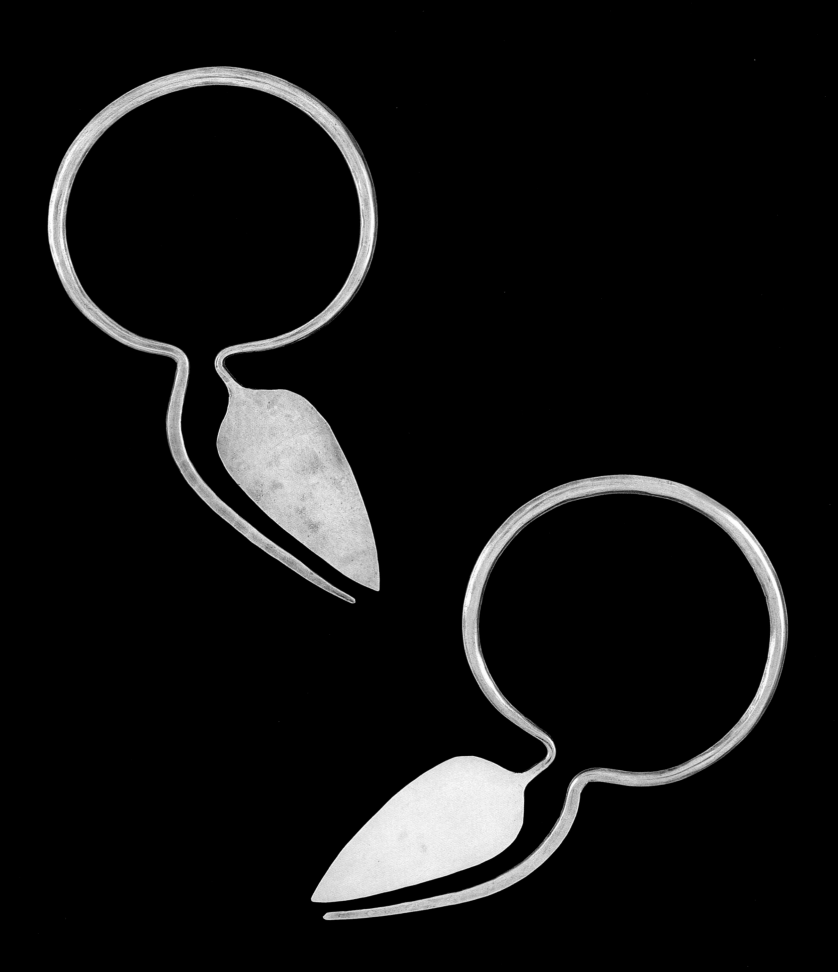

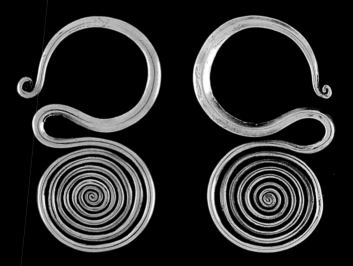

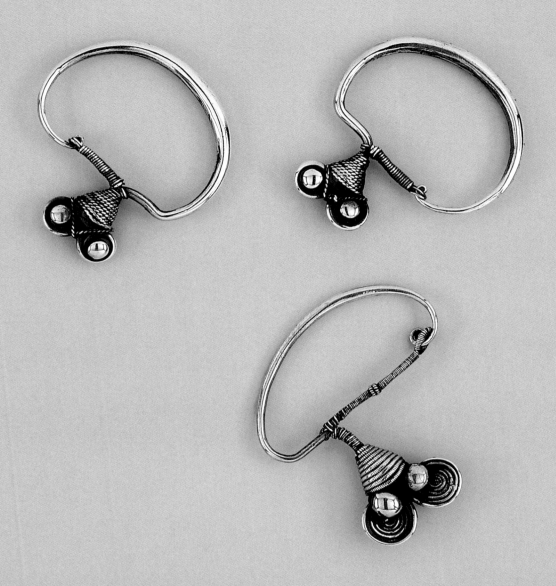

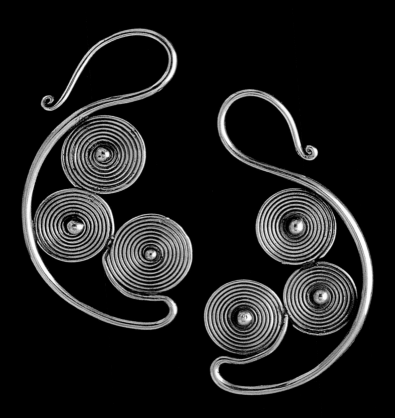

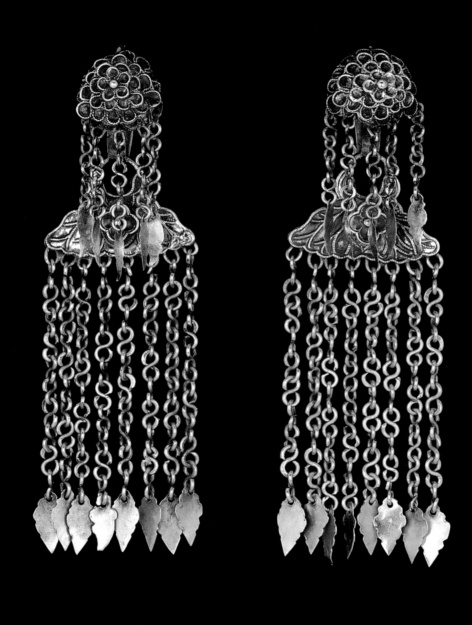

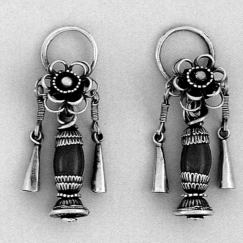

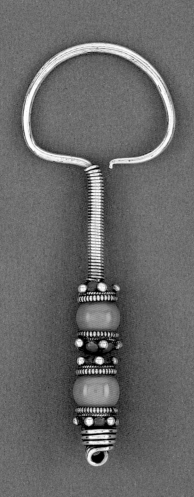

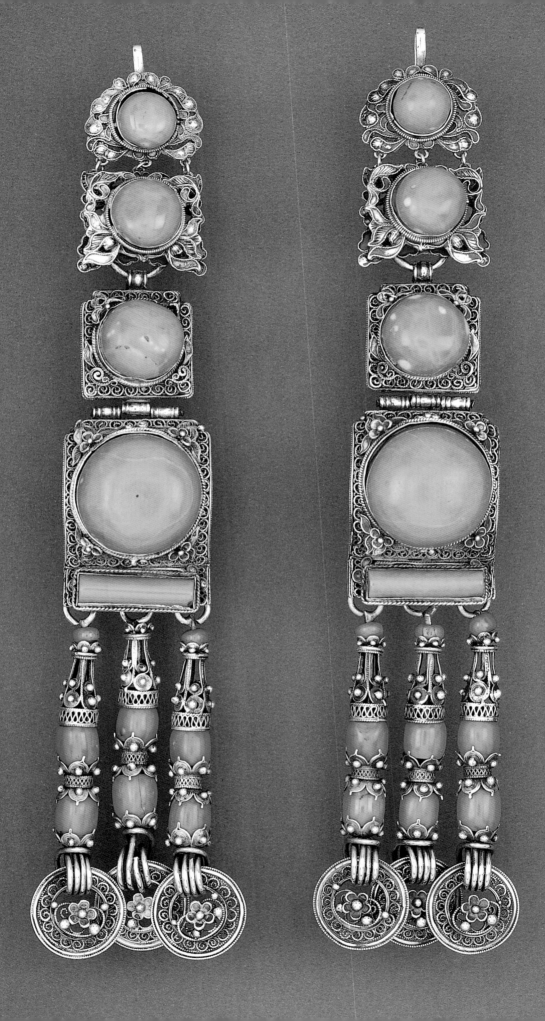

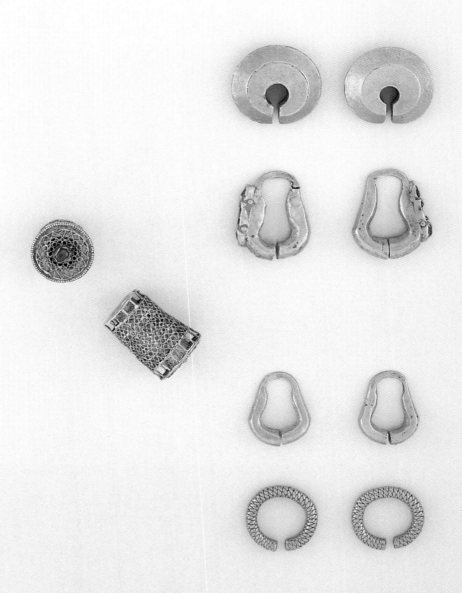

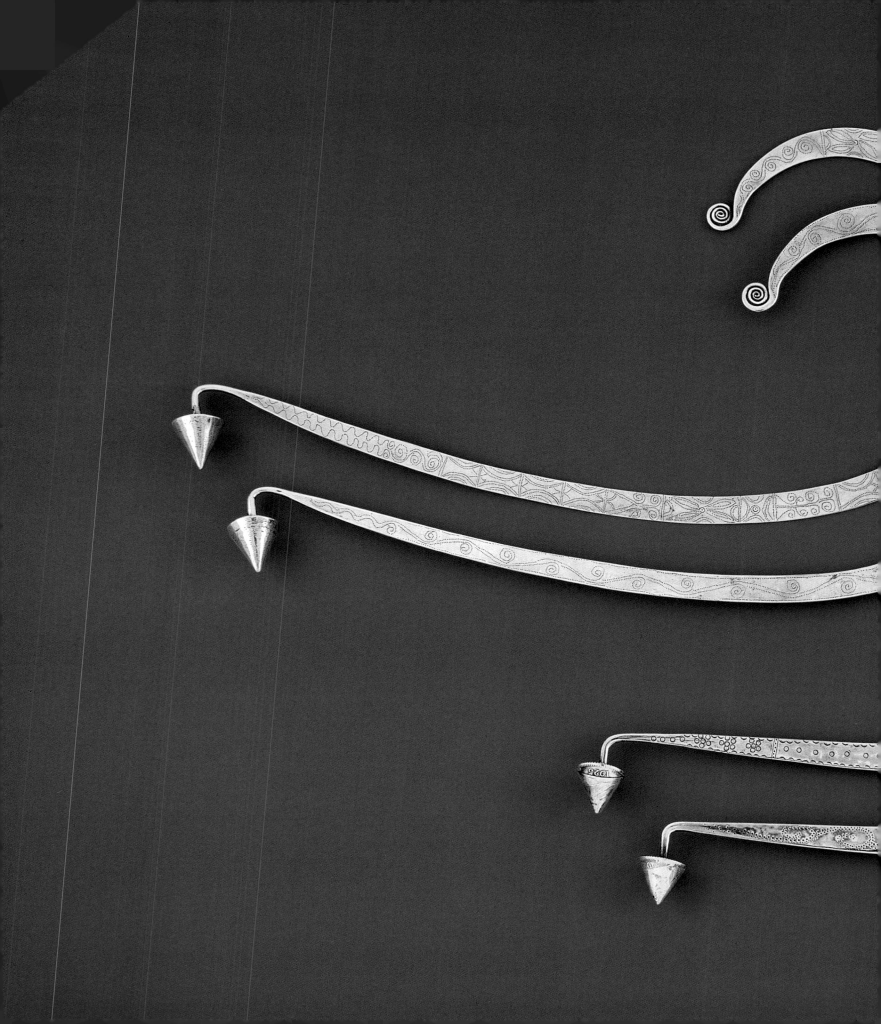

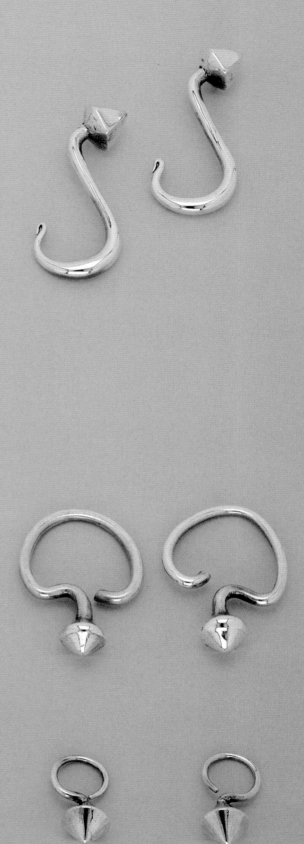

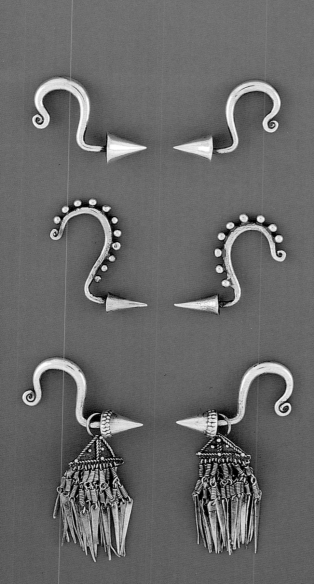
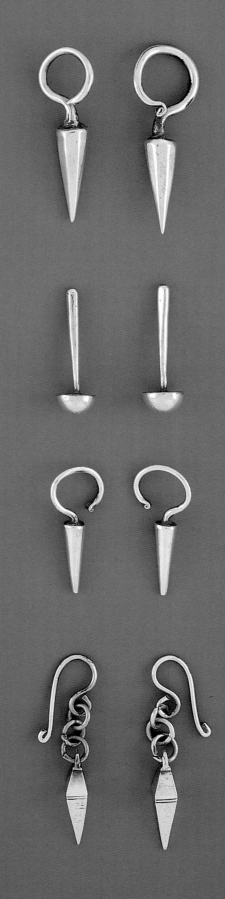

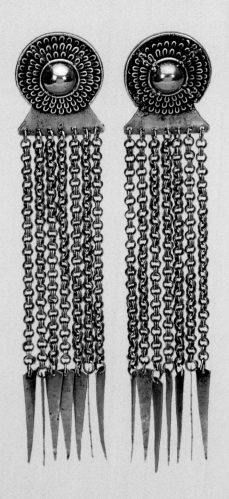

226

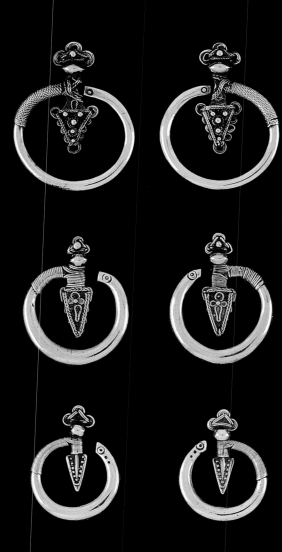

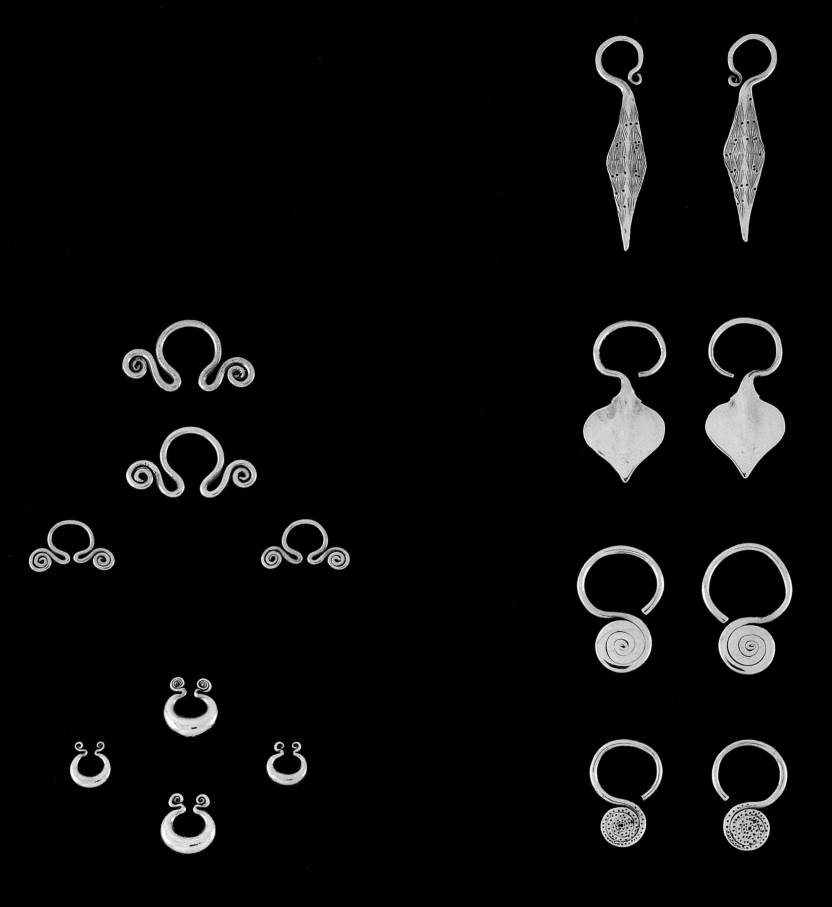

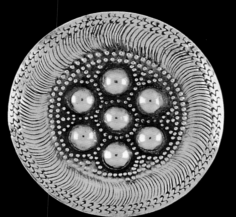

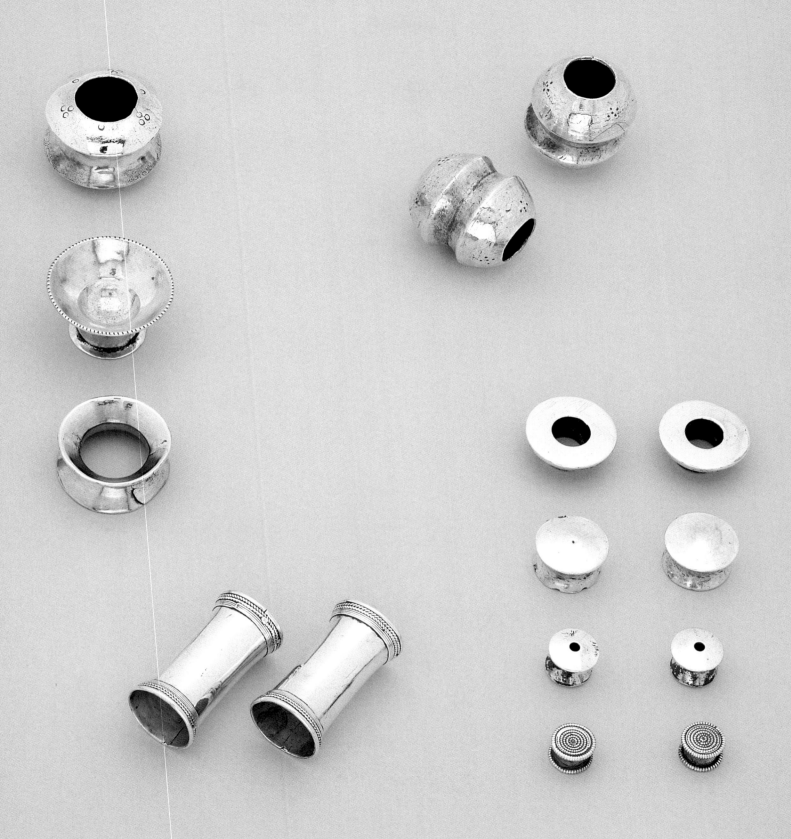

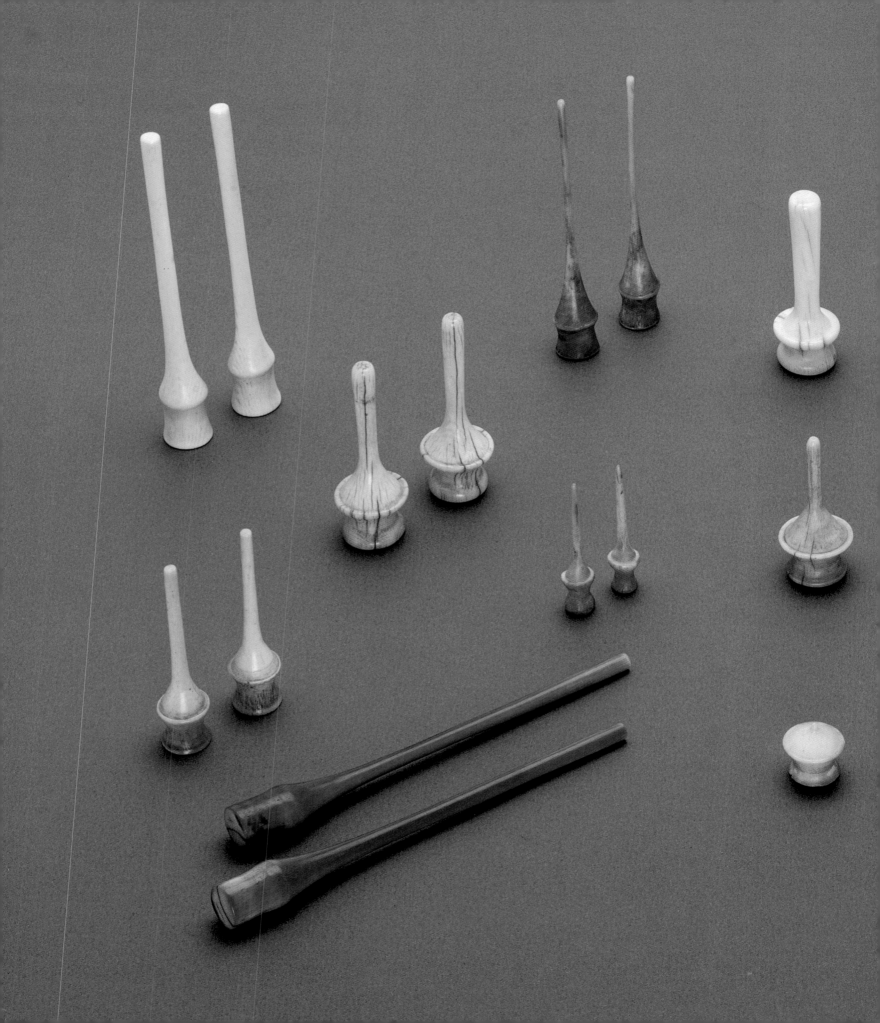

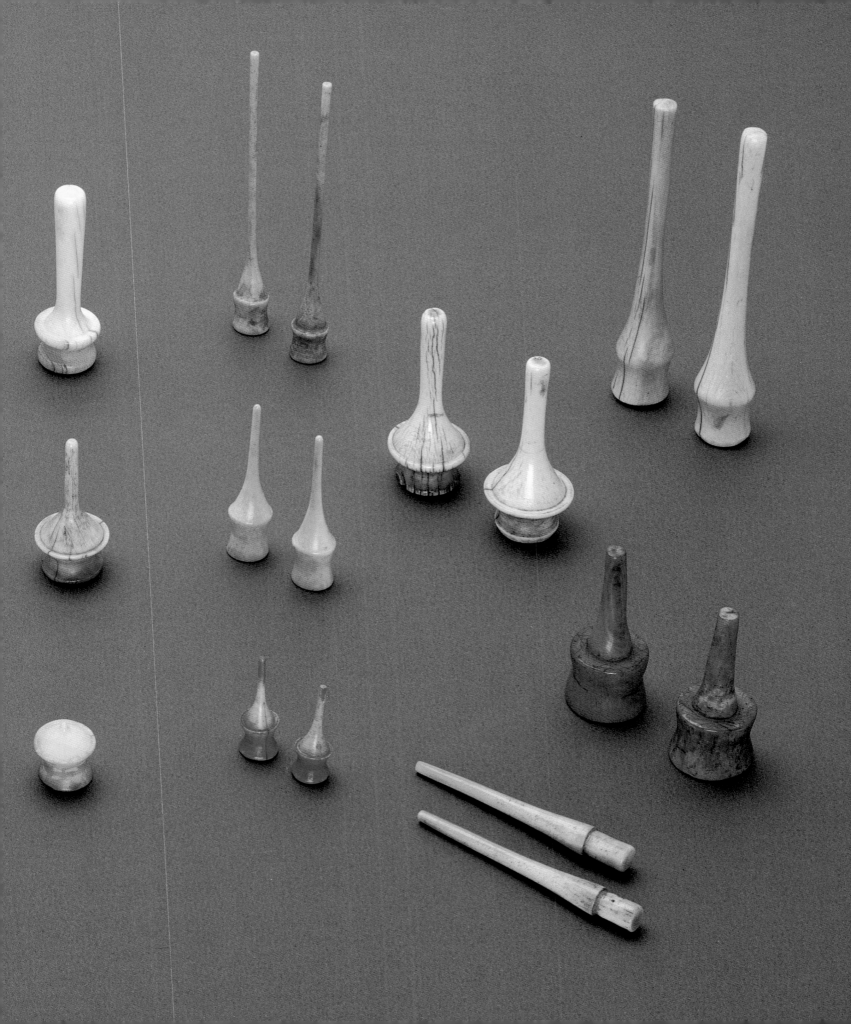

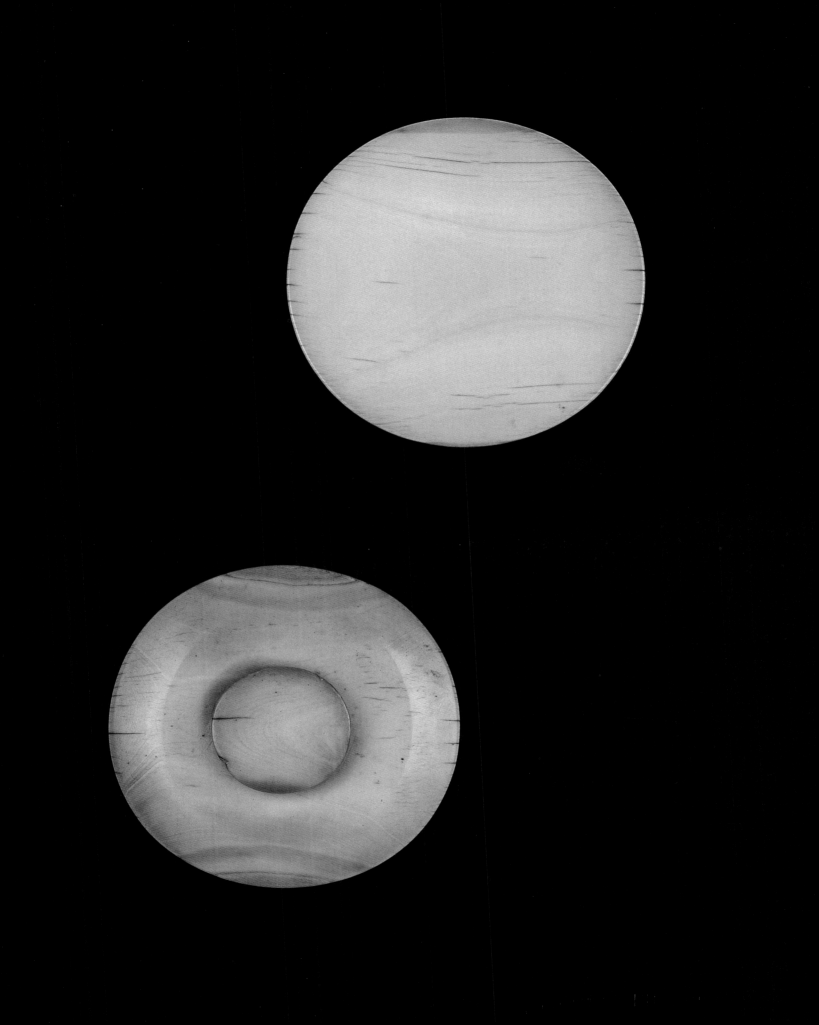

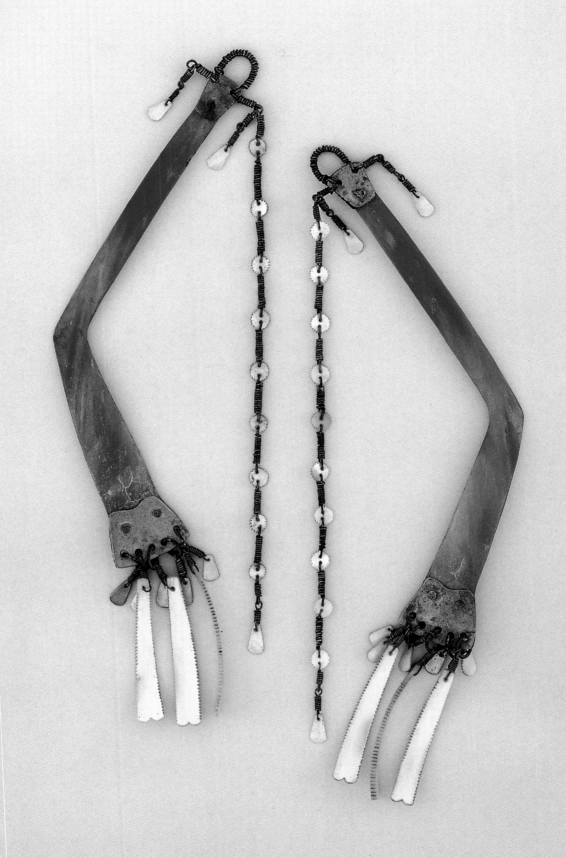

249

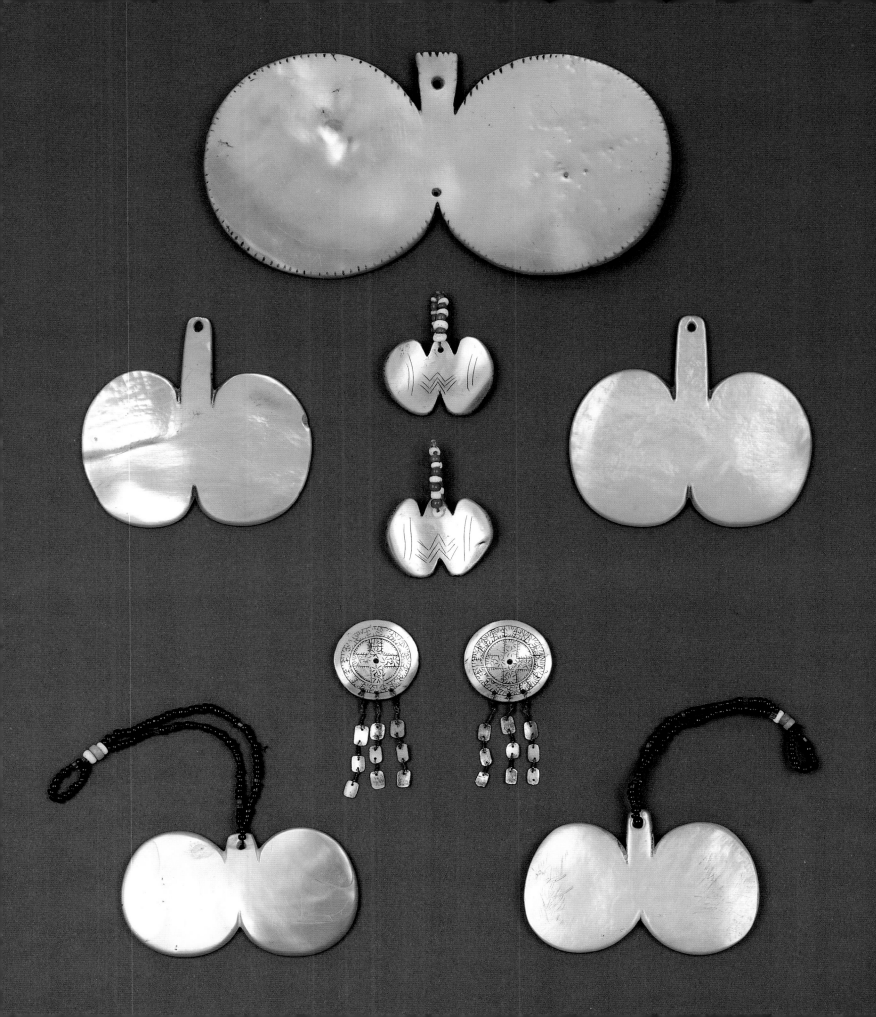

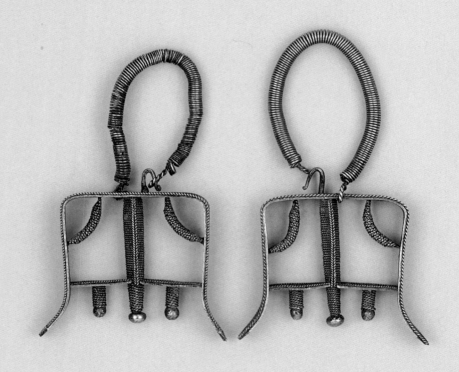

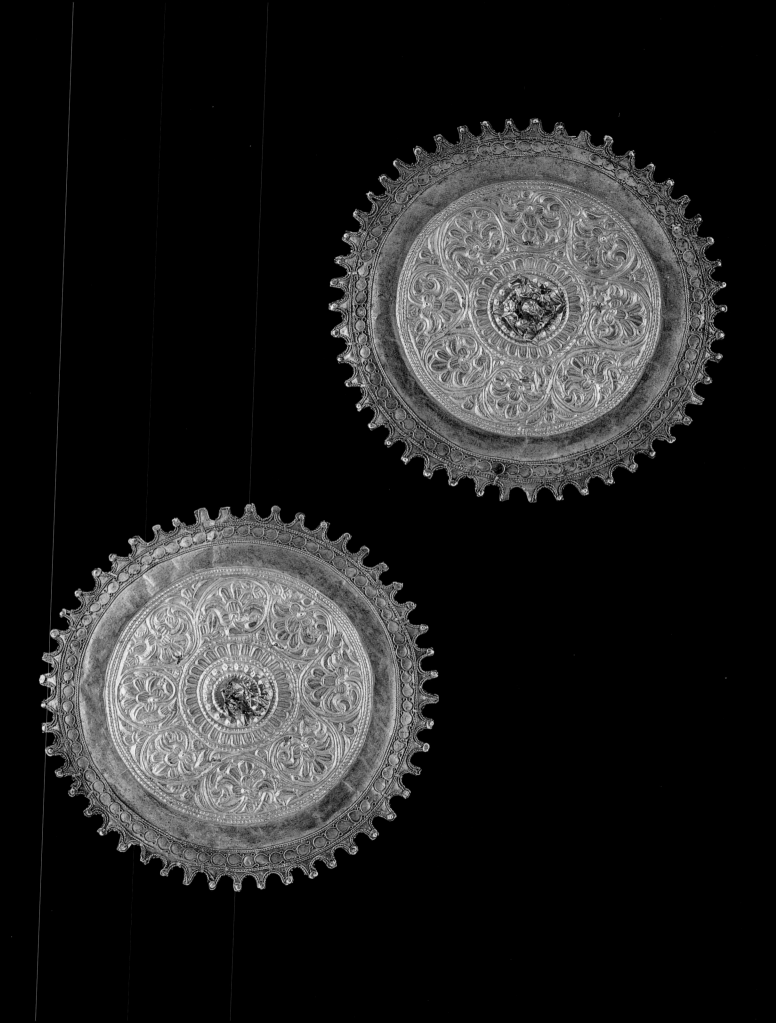

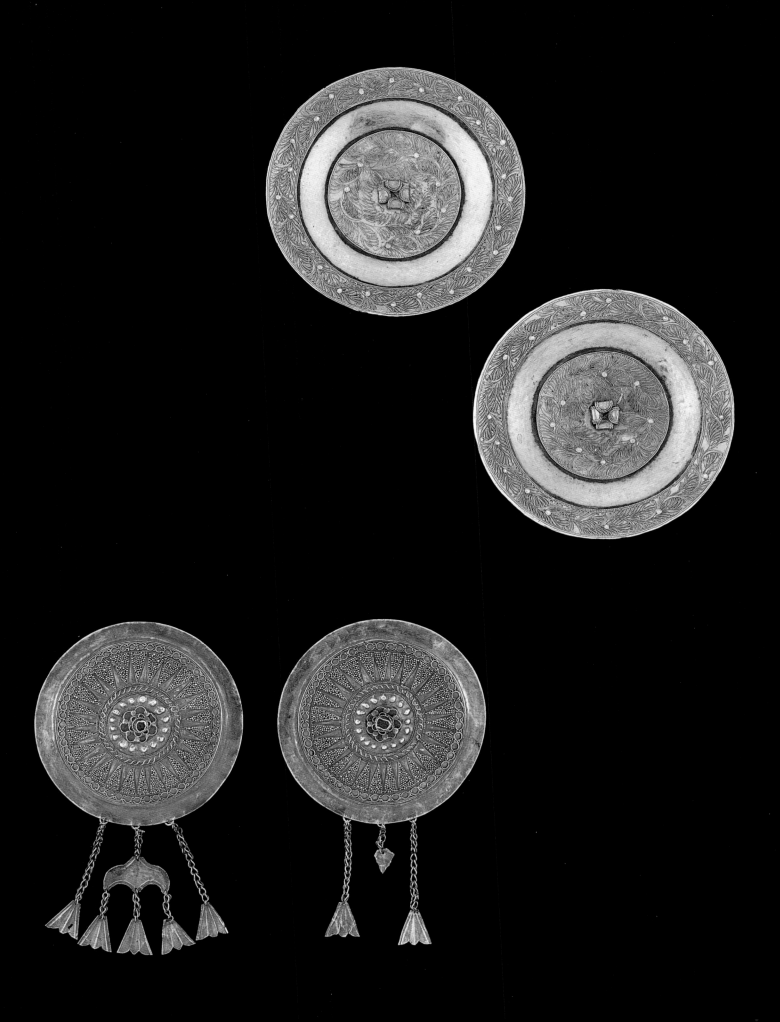

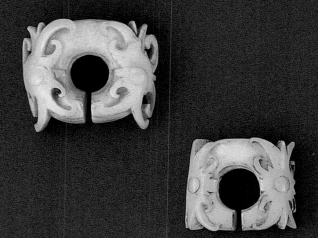

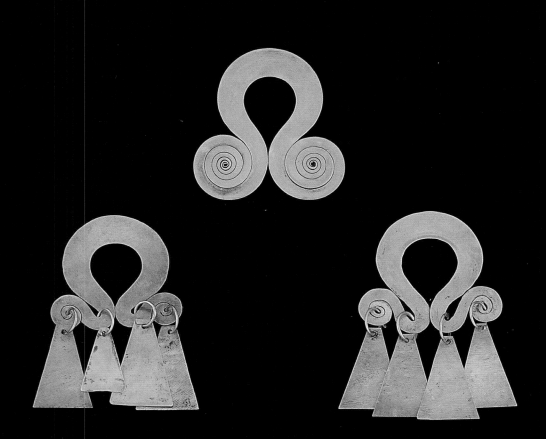

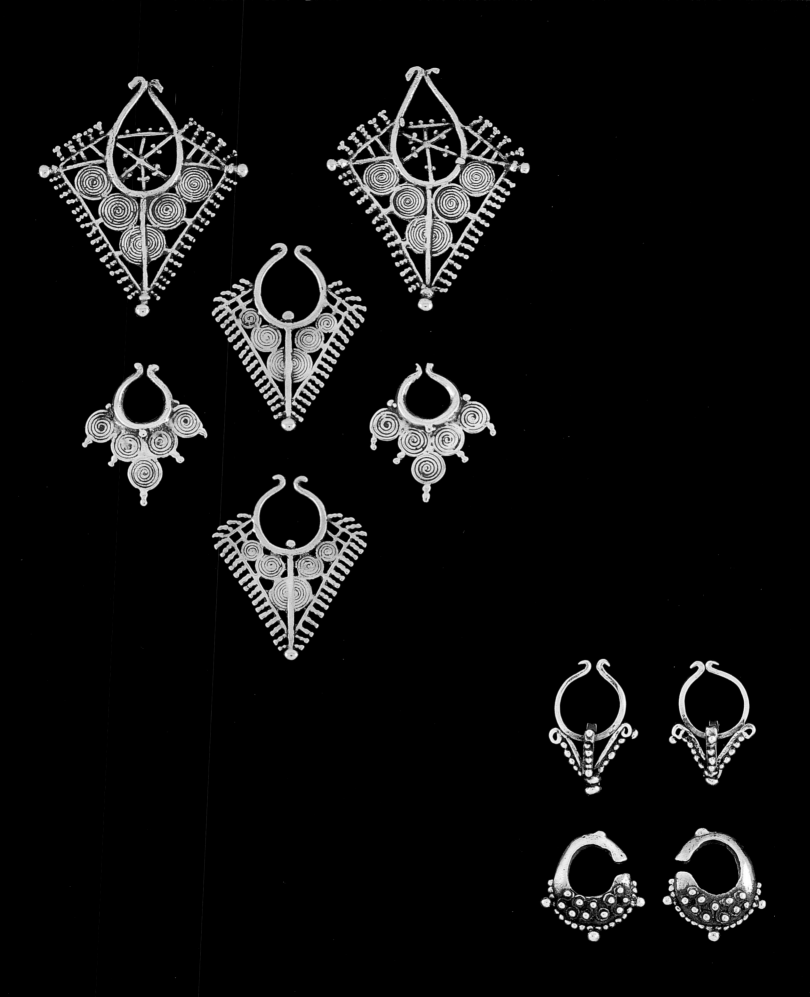

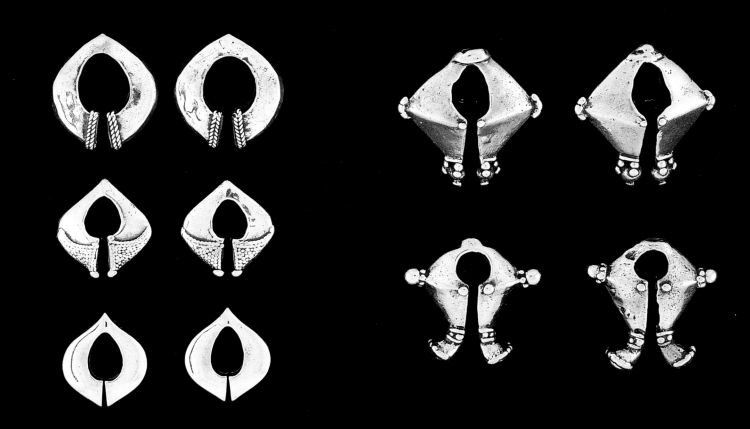
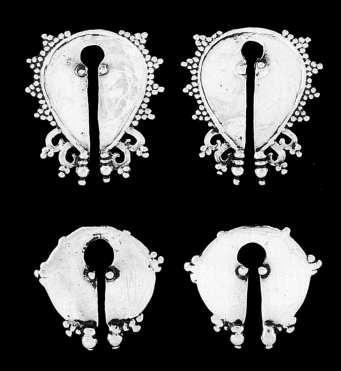

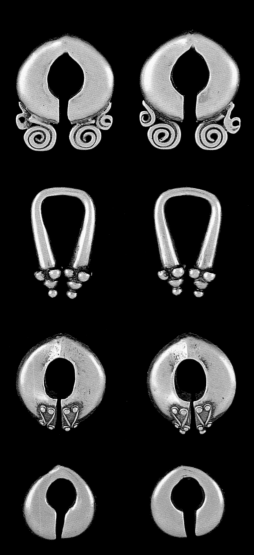

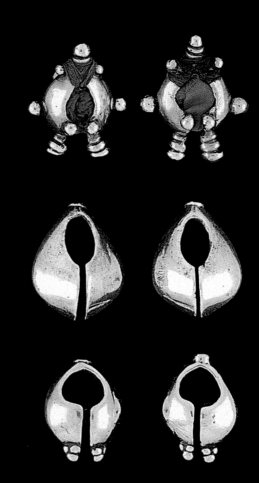
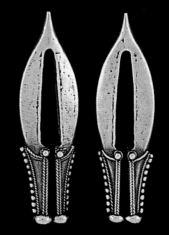

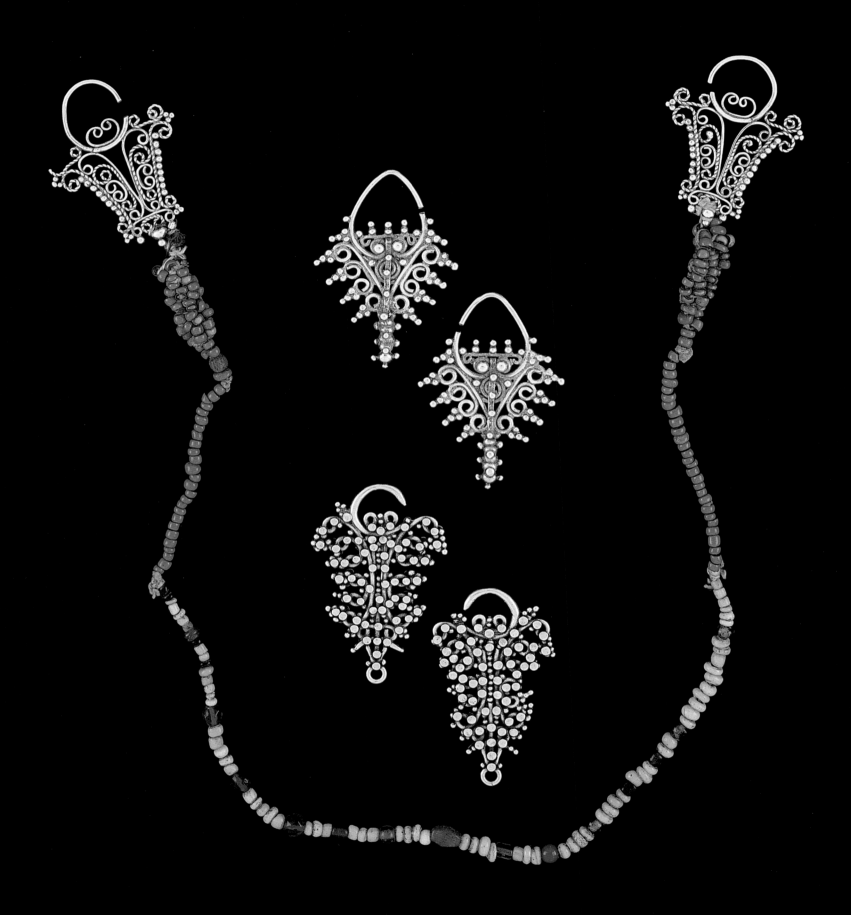

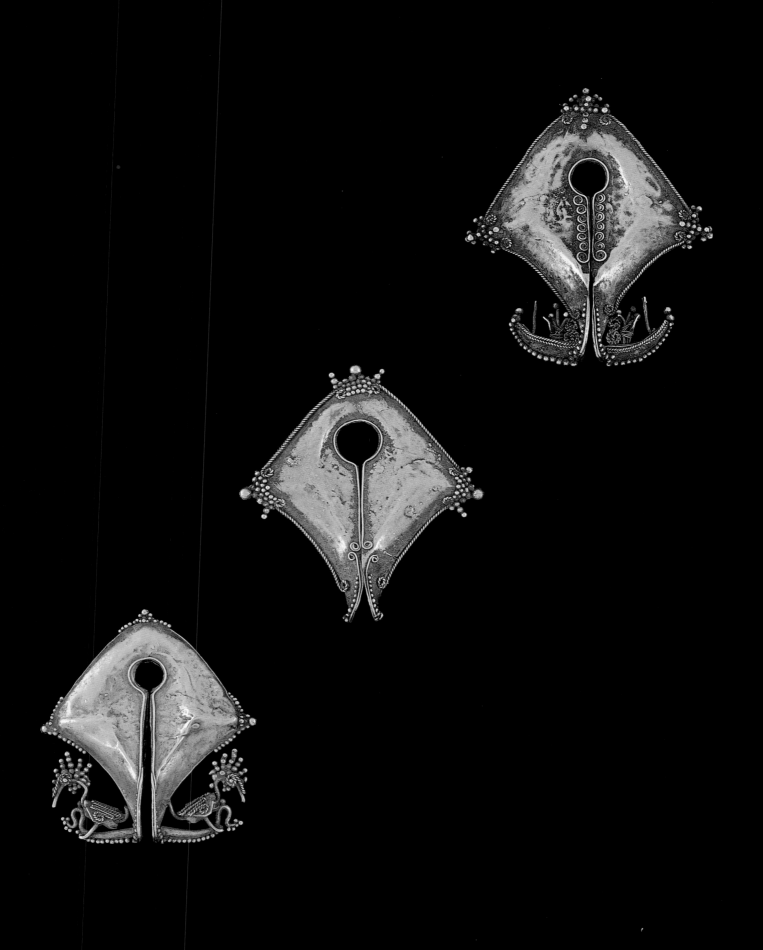

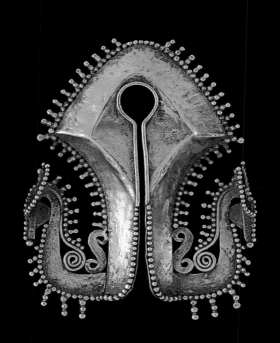

America

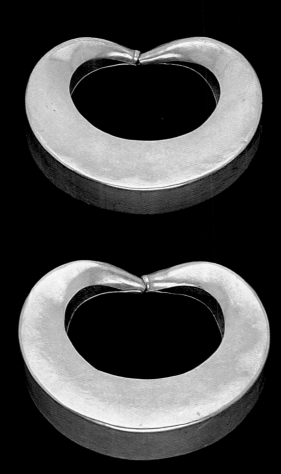

Captions

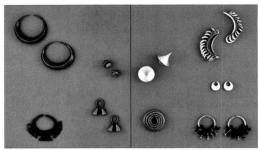   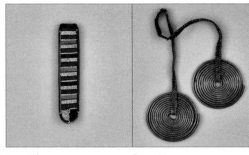

Page 50
Mali (Peul, above);
Cameroon, the studs;
Burkina Faso (Lobi, below
left*)* and *Kenya (Masai,*
the pair below*)*
Bronze and copper.
W. 6.5 cm
The flat earring was found
during an excavation.
Those above are worn by
women, the little copper
pair is worn by men.

Page 51
*Mali (*below right,
Sarakole, above right*),*
Kenya (Kamba, above, left,
Nandi, below left,
Turkana, in the centre*)*
Brass, glass paste, silver
and aluminium.
H. 6.5 cm
The Kamba, like the
Turkana and the Borana,
have used aluminium
since about 1920.

Page 52
Kenya (Samburu), above,
Cameroon, above right,
Sudan (Dinka) and
Burkina Faso (Lobi)
Ivory. W. 6.1 cm
Worn singly or in pairs,
hoops are the distinctive
mark of the Samburu
warrior. Dinka men and
women set much store by
ivory that they salvage
fragments of bracelets and
carve them into earrings.

Lobi ornaments, rather
unusual, are never found
in pairs.

Page 53
Kenya (Masai)
Poker-worked ivory.
H. 16.5 cm
In the past, only Masai
warriors had the right to
wear similar single
ornaments in their
distended ear lobes.

Page 54
Kenya (Masai)
Leather and glass beads.
H. 19.3 cm
Married women are
supposed to wear their ear
flaps at all times; such
items rarely form a pair.
Over time, brightly
coloured beads, imported
from Europe, replaced the
use of local seeds and iron
beads, which were more
difficult to work.

Page 55
Kenya (Masai)
Brass and leather.
Diam. 10.2 cm
In the nineteenth century
women wore heavy iron
ornaments. Some ethnic
groups stripped brass wire
from the telegraph lines
installed by colonial
authorities and craftsmen
used it to make various
types of earrings.

 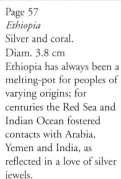 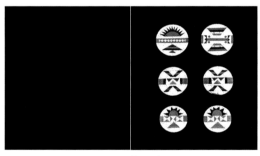

Page 56
Ethiopia, Harer
Silver. H. 8.3 cm
Large beads, made of two
soldered hemispheres, are
evidence of Arab
influence, and indeed the
ancestors of the present-
day inhabitants of Harar
were Arab settlers, who
built up the city.

Page 57
Ethiopia
Silver and coral.
Diam. 3.8 cm
Ethiopia has always been a
melting-pot for peoples of
varying origins; for
centuries the Red Sea and
Indian Ocean fostered
contacts with Arabia,
Yemen and India, as
reflected in a love of silver
jewels.

Page 59
South Africa (Zulu)
Wood, vinyl and nails.
Diam. 6.2 cm
One recurrent motif is
that of the rising sun,
copied from the *Sunbeam
Polish* trademark.
Occasionally, plugs are
decorated on both sides,
like the pair shown here
above.

Asia

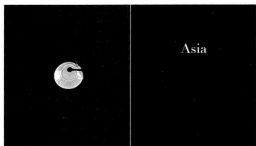 

Page 60
Indonesia
Gold. Diam. 3.3 cm
This split ornament, found during an excavation, derives from an extremely ancient tradition in South-East Asia. In the Moluccas, in eastern Indonesia, this same form was still found in the twentieth century.

Pages 72-73
Oman (Bedouin)
Silver. H. 26.7 cm
The temple ornaments shown in the centre are given particular charm by the mass of hoops and lengthy chains, with very fine mesh. The granulated pear-shaped elements of the *halaq* earring to the extreme left is suggestive of a blackberry. Found at Ur as early as the third millennium BC, this symbol of fecundity is still used in Central Asia and India. Young girls often wear several pairs of such ornaments fixed in their ear lobes or suspended from a chain running over their head.

 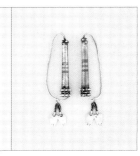

Page 74
Yemen (Bedouin)
Silver, glass paste, cotton and wire. H. 22.5 cm
Traces of gilding are visible. The slightly rough appearance of the suspension hooks contrasts with the finely executed granulation.

Page 75
Oman (Bedouin)
Silver. H. 19 cm
These *nisa* are worn by settled Bedouin women; the better-off may wear several pairs at a time, attached to a headdress made of cloth, leather or silver.

Page 76
Yemen (Bedouin)
Silver and enamel. H. 21 cm
The Muslim consider the triangle a symbol of femininity. Noteworthy is the variety and quality of chains in the Arabic peninsula. The manual manufacturing process of these chains is quite complex.

Page 77
Yemen (Bedouin)
Silver. H. 5.4 cm
Yemeni goldsmiths specialise in filigree and granulation. Jewish craftsmen enjoy a high reputation, as in the Maghreb, and are particularly esteemed for the delicacy and precision of their rendering of detail.

Page 78
Oman (Bedouin)
Silver and gold. H. 12.5 cm
Hilaq like these are the type most commonly found in Northern Oman.

Page 79
Oman (Bedouin)
Silver and gold. H. 12.6 cm
This type of ear pendant was known in Assyria in the eighth century B.C. The *lamiya*, which probably originated in Dhahira, is also found in Sharqiyah and the Emirates. The application of gold leaf is a speciality of the city of Sur.

Page 80
Central Asia (Turkmen, Tekke)
Fire-gilded silver and cornelian. H. 17 cm
These anthropomorphic *Adamlyk* are worn by young girls. The word *adam* was introduced in the language by the Muslim clergy in the sixteenth century, to work out the clan's chiefs genealogy by dating them back to Adam, their first ancestor.

Page 81
Central Asia (Turkmen, Tekke)
Fire-gilded silver and cornelian. H. 21 cm
These *tenecir* – whose triangular form implies protection – may be hung from the ear lobe, from a band of leather, or from the headdress.

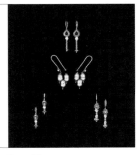

Page 82
Central Asia, Khorezm (Yomud)
Silver and cornelian.
W. 11.2 cm
In the nineteenth century, the Yomud of the north wore *gulak chalka* measuring 12-18 cm.

Page 83
Iran (Yomud)
Silver, silver-gilt and glass.
W. 8.5 cm
The suspension ring on the two upper pairs emerges from dragons' heads, which are regarded as offering protection. The motif of the two back-to-back peacocks, in the centre of the lower earrings, dates back to the Sassanid period.

Page 84
Central Asia, Bukhara (Uzbek)
Silver with gilding traces.
H. 4,4 cm
Traces of floral motifs and a crescent moon are visible on these particularly delicate earrings.

Page 85
Central Asia, Fergana valley, and Afghanistan (Turkmen)
Gold and glass. H. 7 cm
The central earrings are reminiscent of a model from pre-Islamic Iran, which spread throughout the Islamic world of the first Caliphs. The ones with scrolls of twisted wire, are wrongly regarded as being of Kazakh origin.

Pages 86-87
Central Asia, Khanate of Bukhara
Gold, emerald root, tourmaline and baroque pearls.
H. 7.1 and 12.5 cm
In Islamic countries, the colour green – that of the plant world, and of paradise – is particularly favoured. The peacock's tail at the base of the hoop is a cosmic symbol, alluding to the universe, the sun at its zenith, and the full moon.

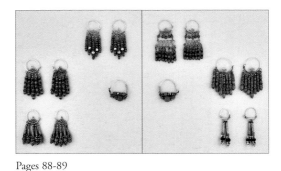

Pages 88-89
Central Asia, Bukhara (Uzbek and Tajik, below right*).*
Women are particularly fond of *chalka* in silver and pale coral. Granulated beads of the type shown here date back to antiquity in Mesopotamia.

Page 90
Central Asia (Uzbek)
Silver, enamel, coral and pearls. H. 8.5 cm
For women who live in towns, whose possessions take the form of real estate and businesses, jewels are worn in order to impress; nomad women on the other hand regard them as talismanic, and as a form of capital which may be easily converted into cash and carried.

Page 91
Central Asia, Bukhara
Silver, silver-gilt, coral and glass paste. H. 9.5 cm
The stylised birds derive from pre-Islamic Sassanian motifs. Generally speaking, ear pendants from the *khanates* of Central Asia convey a sense of great femininity and are a remarkable tribute to the immense sophistication of the art produced in Central Asian oases.

Page 92
Central Asia, Khiva
Fire-gilded silver, tourmaline, turquoise and glass. H. 13.2 cm
These ear pendants form a parure with a matching pectoral and temple ornaments. The often elaborate jewels worn in the towns contrast strikingly with those worn by nomadic women, which are extremely austere. Both faces of each earring are set with a central piece of glass of a different colour.

Page 93
Central Asia, Samarkand
Silver, enamel, coral, glass paste and turquoise.
H. 29 cm
These temple ornaments, *mokhi tillo*, are a harmonious combination of perfectly executed enamelling, beautifully regular chains, and stamped pendants. The Iranian turquoise owes its reputation to its durability, density and hardness. Its name, *firuze*, derives from *firuz*, victory, of which it is the symbol.

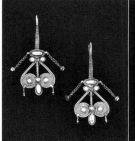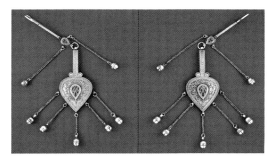

Page 94
Central Asia (Kazakh)
Silver. H. 15.5 cm
Expert opinion is divided
as to the origins of these
ear pendants. Researchers
from the Museum of
Oriental Art in Moscow
came upon similar ones
during an expedition to
Kazakhstan in 1977, but
Western experts attribute
them to the Turkmen of
Iran.

Page 95
*Central Asia, Kazakhstan
and Pakistan, Nuristan,*
centre and below
Silver. H. 11.7 cm
These pendants, in rolled
silver, have punched
decoration.

Pages 96-97
Central Asia (Kazakh)
Silver, fire-gilded silver-gilt
and coloured glass.
H. 32,5 cm
These *shekkelik*, stamped
with fake granulation, are
part of the nuptial parure.

Page 98
Central Asia (Tajik)
Nielloed silver, coral and
glass paste. H. 14 cm
The basic form of these
chalka is the crescent
moon, which is associated
with femininity. Glass
paste is a substitute for
turquoise, whose symbolic
value is linked to its
colour.

Page 99
Central Asia (Kirghiz)
Silver, enamel and coral.
H. 22 cm
Unlike Tibetan women,
the women of the oases
prefer pale coral. The
tinkling of the chains is
said to frighten spirits.
The little pendants are
stamped.

Page 100
Central Asia (Kirghiz)
Silver, enamel and coral.
H. 8.5 cm

Page 101
Central Asia (Kirghiz)
Silver and coral. H. 11 cm
The dome-like shape of
these *gushwar-e kafasi*,
formerly regarded as of
Kazakh workmanship, is
reminiscent of a bird cage,
as their name implies. The
upper motif on the pair
shown below suggests a
bird in flight.

Page 102
Central Asia (Kirghiz)
Silver and coral. H. 9 cm
The motif within the
hoop probably symbolises
the full moon instead of
the sun.

Page 103
*Afghanistan or Pakistan,
south of Peshawar*
Silver-gilt and glass.
H. 7.5 cm
The region where these
repoussé pendants were
made was strongly
influenced by Indian art.
The red glass is an allusion
to Surya, the sun.

Page 104
Afghanistan
Gold. H. 10 cm
Fruits and seeds are
regarded as protecting
against the evil eye. The
early-flowering almond
tree alludes to the rebirth
of nature.

Page 105
*Central Asia, Afghanistan
and Fergana valley*
Gold. H. 4.8 cm
Such earrings, finely
executed in openwork
filigree, are a variant of the
basic type found
throughout the Islamic
world, and have
similarities with those of
Iran and Kurdistan.

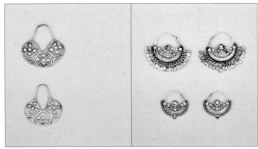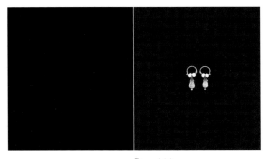

Page 106
Pakistan, Nuristan, Waigal valley
Silver. H. 8.5 cm
The particular appeal of these earrings lies in their combination of formal simplicity and *repoussé* decoration.

Page 107
Pakistan (Pashtun)
Silver and mica.
H. 8.8. cm
The extremely harsh existence led by the nomad women of Sind leaves them few resources to devote to sets of ornaments.

Page 108
Pakistan
Silver-gilt, glass beads and cotton. H. 12 cm
The cluster of pendants makes an effective contrast with the alternating play of voids and solids.

Page 109
Pakistan
Silver-gilt and glass.
H. 13.7 cm
When complete, these *muchley* would have included a double row of little pieces in glass paste around the circumference. The representation of the sun might derive from ancient pre-Islamic cults, or be the result of the influence of nearby India.

Page 111
India, Lucknow
Gold, amber, pearls, enamel and diamond. H. 4.8 cm
Amber symbolises solar, spirtual or divine attraction. The exceptional physical qualities of the diamond make it – here mounted at the base of the amber pearl – the symbol of steadfastness. These extremely sophisticated earrings are an expression of Indian femininity.

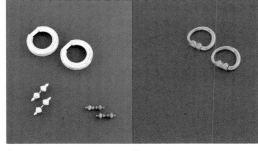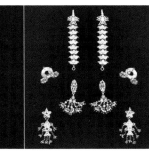

Page 112
India
Ivory and bone, bottom right. Diam. 6.2 cm
The group of frescoes in the temple of Lukhang, which stands in the middle of a lake below the Potala palace at Lhasa in Tibet, illustrates the esoteric practices of the Tibetan tantric tradition. Many of the male figures are shown wearing large hoops, apparently in ivory, similar to the ones shown here.

Page 113
India, Kerala
Gold. W. 5.9 cm
According to Oppi Untracht, *kunuk* were worn in the rim of the ear by Christian Indo-Syrian women. Nowadays they are worn exclusively by older women.

Page 114
India, Gujarat (Rabari)
Gold. H. 7 cm
The upper earrings, and the lozenge-shaped *pandadi*, are decorated with lotus flowers, a symbol of life which may take many forms. The Mehr women decorate their ear lobes with *loriyan* (below), with conspicuously large hoops.

Page 115
India, Gujarat (Rabari)
Gold. H. 8 cm
Double-coned *nagla* are worn by Dhebaria Rabari women; wire *nagla* are worn by married Kachhi Rabari women in their distended ear lobes.

Page 116
India, Orissa
Gold. H. 16.5 cm
These pendants, in very fine filigree, illustrate the immense skill of Indian goldsmiths, despite the rudimentary range of tools at their disposal.

Page 117
North India
Gold, turquoise, precious stones and real pearls.
H. 12 cm
These various types of earrings are designed with a view to enhance the Indian woman's sensuality. Those mounted with precious stones are typical of Mughal workmanship. The *matsya* fish, symbolising water, is an avatar of Vishnu, who saved Manu from the flood.

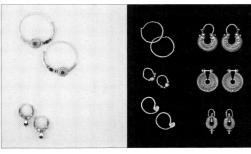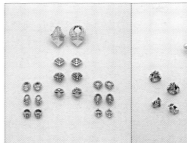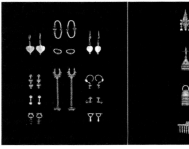

Page 118
India, below, *Himachal Pradesh*
Gold and glass.
H. 7 cm

Page 119
India, Himachal Pradesh, above and below left, *Kutch,* to the right, *Tamil Nadu,* in the centre, to the right. *Rajasthan,* below right.
Gold. H. 5.6 cm

Women wear several pairs of *pandi* hoops, decorated with wire, in the rim of their ears. The crescent-shaped *ogania* are worn exclusively by men, at their weddings, which are celebrated collectively.

Page 120
India, Kerala, above, centre, *Karmataka* and *Tamil Nadu.*
Gold. H. 4.5 cm
The pendants above are worn by Malayalam Muslims. Those in the middle of the bottom blocks suggest a tropical fruit, reference to fecundity. Those on the right, below, represent mount Meru, axis of the world.

Page 121
India, Tamil Nadu
Gold. H. 3.9 cm
The *thandatti* shown above, whose centre has three levels alluding to the three worlds – terrestrial, astral and divine – are linked to the idea of the *mandala,* which indicates the four cardinal points. *Pampadam,* shown below left, are reminiscent of serpents.

Page 122
India, Tamil Nadu the small ones, below, and the oval hoops, above, *Rajasthan,* with chain, and to the right, the two pairs above, *Gujarat* to the left, above, *Karmatala,* the third to the left
Gold and glass. H. 8.5 cm
The two pairs shown above are decorated with cobras and pipal leaves, those of the *Ficus religiosa,* the bo

tree, beneath which Buddha received enlightenment.

Page 123
India, Tamil Nadu, above, *Kerala,* below
Gold. H. 4.7 cm
The upper earrings are hollow. Women from the south of India have a passion for gold and earrings, of which there are an infinite variety.

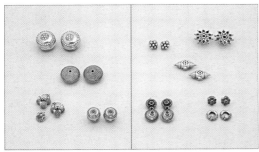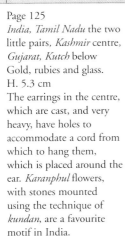

Page 124
India, above and below right *Kerala,* in the centre *Kutch (Vaghadia Rabari)* below left *Rajasthan (Kalbelli)* and *South India*
Gold and precious stones. Diam. 4 cm
Thodda, above and below right, are the emblem of coconut pickers. Married Rabari men decorate the rims of their ears with granulated *bhungari,* and ear lobes with *ogania.* The *gokhru* motif of fruits and seed was known before our era.

Page 125
India, Tamil Nadu the two little pairs, *Kashmir* centre, *Gujarat, Kutch* below
Gold, rubies and glass.
H. 5.3 cm
The earrings in the centre, which are cast, and very heavy, have holes to accommodate a cord from which to hang them, which is placed around the ear. *Karanphul* flowers, with stones mounted using the technique of *kundan,* are a favourite motif in India.

Page 126
India, Karnataka
Gold, glass and pearls.
H. 5 cm
Because of its wheel-shaped open tail, the peacock has become a solar symbol. The little masks on the lower pairs are *kirtimukha.* Sometimes the earrings consist of several connecting parts.

Page 127
India, Karnataka and *Maharashtra*
Gold and real pearls.
H. 8 cm
In India, pearls are credited with healing powers, and are regarded as precious stones. Associated with water, and femininity, they are also a symbol of fecundity. Their delicate piercing requires great skill. The trapezoid earrings and the two small pairs in the centre are worn in the rim of the ear.

Page 128
India, Gujarat, Saurashtra
Gold. H. 7.5 cm
These *panddi,* in rolled gold, have extraordinarily skilful floral decoration in filigree and granulation. Apprentices entered their father's workshops at an extremely early age.

Page 129
India
Silver. H. 5 cm
The particular charm of these ear pendants derives from their exquisite proportions, the play of curves, and the perfect balance between the voids and solids.

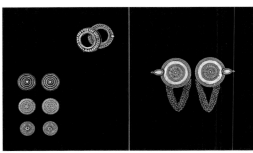
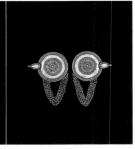
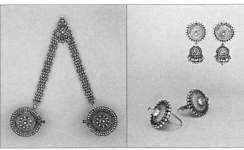
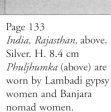

Page 130
India, Gujarat
Silver and silver-gilt.
H.4.9 cm
Women wear these *kundal* ornaments in their distended ear lobes. Examples of the oldest types can be seen in frescoes or on statues. Worked in *repoussé*, they are relatively light. The circumferences of stone discs have been decorated

with birds since the time of the Maurya.

Page 131
India, Madhya Pradesh
Silver. Total height 11 cm
With their discs and radiating rays, these *tarkulia* are a solar symbol, a recurrent motif since the Indus civilization. The Rai women of central Nepal wear identical ornaments, with the projection pointing towards the chin.

Page 132
India, Rajasthan (Bhil)
Silver. H. 25 cm
The weight of such *phuljhumka* is lightened by a chain fixed in the hair.

Page 133
India, Rajasthan, above.
Silver. H. 8.4 cm
Phuljhumka (above) are worn by Lambadi gypsy women and Banjara nomad women.

Page 134
India
Silver, silver-gilt and glass beads. H. 8.4 cm
Tinkling bells ward off harmful spirits. The profusion of bells on the pair shown above, reminiscent of soft roe, is an allusion to fecundity.

Page 135
India, Rajasthan
Silver and turquoise.
H. of hoops 10.3 cm
The peacock is a symbol of beauty and the power of transmutation. Identified with the sun, the element of fire, it has the ability to destroy serpents, associated with the element of water.

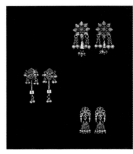

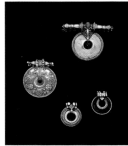
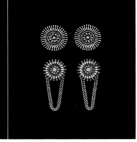

Page 136
India, Himachal Pradesh,
above and below *Gujarat
(Rabari)*
Silver, glass paste and enamel. H. 5.7 cm
Emerging from the darkness, opening up in full sunlight (above), the lotus is the symbol of spiritual blossoming. Its eight petals, like the eight points of space, are suggestive of cosmic harmony. The blue and green enamel on silver is typical of Himachal Pradesh.

Page 137
*India, Himachal Pradesh,
Kulu*
Silver and glass. H. 10 cm
Green and red are frequently combined in Indian jewels. The colour of hope and strength, green is also the colour of immortality; red, the colour of blood, associated with the fire of the sun, is a basic symbol of life.

Page 138
India, Gujarat, Saurashtra
Silver and applications in gilver-gilt. W. 10 cm
Akota are worn in the elongated ear lobes of Rabari, Ahir and Bharwad women. The little *pohkani* from Saurashtra are illustrated from both front and back.

Page 139
India, Delhi, below.
Silver and glass.
Height with chains, 10.2 cm, Diam. 4.6 cm
The *Karanphul* ear studs represent a flower, while those above have a combination of solar and floral motifs.

Page 140
North India
Silver. Diam. 8.5 cm
These flat engraved hoops are given a sense of volume by the cluster of granules. The floral motifs on the lower part, made in a mould, are applied.

Page 141
India, Kashmir, in the centre, *Panjab*, above, *Gujarat*, bottom
Silver and coral. W. 8 cm
While the smooth hoop enclosed in wire is one of the simplest forms of earring, it lends itself to an almost unlimited variety of forms. Bhopa Rabari women decorate the rims of their ears with *khuti* (below).

 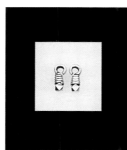  

Page 142
India, Rajasthan (Rabari,
left above and 3rd*), Orissa,*
below left *Kashmir,* above
right *Himachal Pradesh,*
below right
Silver. W. 6 cm
The vast range of types
found in India reflects the
vastness of its territory,
and the thousand-year-old
tradition of the
goldsmith's art itself.

Page 143
India, Gujarat (Rabari)
Silver. H. 8 cm
The Rabari, nomadic
shepherds who live in
Kutch, Saurashtra, Gujarat
and Rajasthan, are divided
into some dozen sub-
groups. The history of their
migrations dates back five
centuries. Rabari women
wear several pairs of
pendants in the lobe and
rims of their ears.

Page 144
*India, Gujarat (Bhopa
Rabari)*
Silver. H. 5.5 cm
Most Rabari earrings are
made of gold or silver.
Vedhla, the oldest type of
Bhopa earrings, are now
worn only by old women.
In India, a large ear lobe is
a sign of strength and
vitality.

Page 145
India, Orissa (Badaga)
Silver. H. 5.3 cm
Nagula, in the form of a
spiralling cobra, are fixed to
the circumference of the
ear and passed through
four or five holes, according
to the number of spirals. In
India, women who want a
child sometimes adopt a
cobra. The helicoidal spiral
is suggestive of the repeated
rhythms of life itself.

Page 146
*India, Nagaland (Konyak
Naga)*
Wood, glass paste,
vegetable fibre and goat's
hair. H. 41 cm
These ornaments are the
badge of headhunters. The
hair is dyed with madder
root, using the process
known as *ikat.* The Naga
are great lovers of pearls,
and very demanding as to
their quality.

Page 147
India, Nagaland
Brass and orchid fibre.
H. 5.5 cm
Orchids abound and are
greatly prized for the
yellow colour of their
stems. Young Ao boys,
who are allowed to adorn
themselves only with wild
flowers, wear orchids in
their ear lobes.

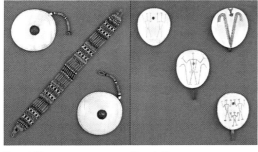  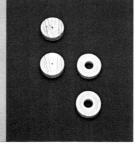 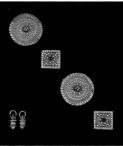 

Page 148
*Inda, Nagaland (Konyak
Naga)*
Shell, brass and glass
beads. Diam. 7 cm,
chin-piece 32.5 cm
The shells are linked by the
beaded chin-piece. Since
the territory occupied by
the Naga is very far from
the sea, and the nearest
market where shells can be
purchased is in Calcutta,
shell ornaments are a sign
of wealth and rank. Beads
could formerly be
purchased at Manipur, or
from travelling traders.

Page 149
*India, Nagaland (Konyak
Naga)*
Shell, *Xancus,* bamboo
and glass beads. H. 8 cm
Worn exclusively by
headhunters, these
ornaments are decorated
with anthropomorphic
motifs, and with the
tattooed V (reminiscent of
buffalo horns) worn on
the chests of warriors
wishing to increase their
vital energy.

Page 150
India, Nagaland (Ao Naga)
Glass and cotton.
Diam. 6 cm
These ornaments are worn
by women. Earrings of the
type shown below may
sometimes be of rock
crystal.

Page 151
India, Nagaland (Naga)
Ivory. Diam. 5.2 cm
Elephants do not enter
Naga territory unless
driven by hunger, and the
Naga rarely hunt them.
From the nineteenth
century onwards traders
from the plains and from
Calcutta provided them
with ivory. Men wear
these plugs in their ear
lobes.

Page 152
Nepal (Tamang)
Gold, turquoise, coral and
glass. Diam. 6.5 cm
These earrings are inserted
into the outer ear by
means of a tube. Since
they are embossed, large
studs like the ones shown
here do not require much
raw material, as the gold
leaf rests on a filling of
pitch.

Page 153
*Nepal (Gurung and
Tamang)*
Gold. Diam. 7.6 cm
Since it is difficult to
insert these *cheptisun* into
the stretched ear lobe they
are often sealed for good
by the goldsmith.
Nowadays, women prefer
smaller hoops requiring
less gold. The main motif
is the sun and a crescent
moon.

Page 154
Tibet
Silver and turquoise.
H. 8.6 cm
Ekbor pendants in
turquoise mosaic work are
fixed in pierced ear lobes or
at the height of the temple,
in women's headdresses.
Men and women wear the
aylong shown in the centre,
in gold, silver or brass, set
with a large turquoise or
several smaller ones.

Page 155
Tibet, Kham
Silver and turquoise.
H. 13 cm
Highly prized *gyu*
turquoises are classified
according to colour.
Women build up a stock
of them until they have
enough matching stones to
make a jewel.

Pages 156-157
Tibet
Silver, turquoise and coral.
H. 9.7 and 8 cm
When a turquoise which
had been blessed by a
lama changed colour or
lost its lustre, prayers had
to be said for the soul of
its owner. Earrings with a
large number of pieces of
coral, above left, and
below right, are worn
exclusively by Amdo

women. *So byis* ear
pendants decorated with
mosaic work in turquoise,
and a piece of coral, above
right, are also worn by
men in the left ear. The
hoop with three stones,
below right, is suggestive
of the *triratna*, the triple
jewel, implying obedience
to the three basic
components of Buddhism.

Page 158
Tibet, Amdo
Silver, enamel, turquoise
and coral. H. 8 cm
The influence of nearby
China can be sensed in
the design of these
women's earrings.

Page 159
Tibet
Gold and turquoise.
Diam. 4.4 cm
Golden *aylong* of this
quality are worn
exclusively by the elite.
Like certain *gau*, these
gold ear studs might
possibly represent the
mandala, with a centre,
the four cardinal points
and the intermediary ones.

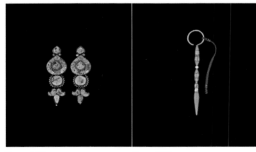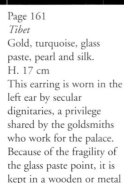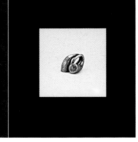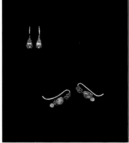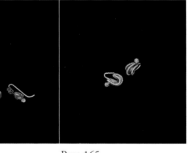

Page 160
Tibet, Lhasa
Gold and turquoise.
H. 12 cm
These ear pendants are
worn by women on festive
occasions. Similar ones
can be seen among the
offerings made by
devotees on the tomb of
the Dalai Lama Thubten
Gyatso.

Page 161
Tibet
Gold, turquoise, glass
paste, pearl and silk.
H. 17 cm
This earring is worn in the
left ear by secular
dignitaries, a privilege
shared by the goldsmiths
who work for the palace.
Because of the fragility of
the glass paste point, it is
kept in a wooden or metal
case.

Page 162
Tibet
Shell and leather.
Diam. 7.7 cm
This rare ornament may
be worn only by Lamaist
priests, though they
generally are pleased with
a small shell hoop, an
emblem of knowledge.
The spiral, which is
naturally formed by the
Xancus, is suggestive of the
formation of a force.

Page 163
China
Silver. H. 4.2 cm
This ornament, in
wrought silver, was found
during excavations.

Page 164
China
God and turquoise.
H. 5 cm
These earrings have the
typical sophistication of
work made during the
Tang dynasty (618-907),
when the arts reached
their zenith and the
empire was at its most
extension.

Page 165
China
Gold. H. 4 cm
Emblems of the
aristocracy, refined yet
sturdy, these pendants
date from the Mongol
dynasty of the Liao, who
invaded China in 947 and
remained in power until
1125.

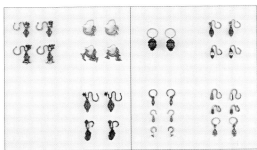

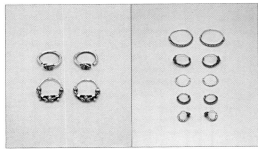

Pages 166-167
China, Ming dynasty (1368-1644)
Silver-gilt and jade. H. 4.2 and 4.5 cm
Trade, and the arts in general, were at their most flourishing under the Ming dynasty. The dragon, whether suggested by the inverted S-shape of various pendants, or emerging more explicitly (left), is the emblem of the emperor. Because of its longevity, the carp is an auspicious symbol; since it swims upstream, it is associated with courage and perseverance. According to Tcheou Touen-yi, the lotus symbolises purity, as well as sobriety and rectitude. The lower pairs shown on the two columns on the left-hand page represent fruits, while those on the right are "hands of Buddha".

Pages 168-169
China, Xingiang (Uigur and Kirghiz)
Silver and gold. H. 7 and 5.3 cm
The half-moon, and the techniques of filigree and granulation widely used in Islamic art, are also found in work from this region.

Page 170
China (Dong)
Silver. H. 5 cm
Dong and Miao co-exist as chief minorities in the same provinces of the South-West.

Page 171
China (Dong)
Silver. Diam. 4.6 cm

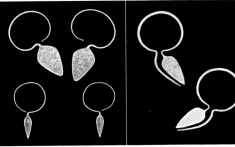

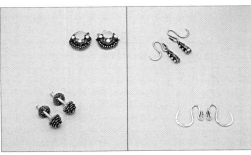

Pages 172-173
China, Guizhou (Dong)
Silver, brass and jade. H. 14 and 5.4 cm
One single type of hoop may or may not be accompanied by various types of pendants. The small pairs shown above and below have stylised dragons' heads.

Pages 174-175
China, Guizhou (Miao)
Silver. H. 14.5 and 15.5 cm
The Yi of Yunnan wear earrings similar to the small engraved pair shown here. The larger ones are also worn by the Lao Lan Tien of Laos. Many ear pendants show a pronounced feeling for form. When dressed for special occasions, young girls are positively bowed down under the mass of their baroque-style silver ornaments, which may weigh up to ten kilograms.

Page 176
China (Miao)
Silver and enamel. H. 6.3 cm
The plant kingdom is a recurrent source of inspiration for such ornaments.

Page 177
China (Miao)
Silver. H. 7 cm
The form is suggestive of the dragon which, as a demonic symbol, is associated with the *naga* serpent. As the guardian of hidden treasures, it must be killed before such treasures can be reached. Combining positive and negative aspects, the dragon is regarded as ambivalent, which is why two confronted dragons are often seen in Oriental art.

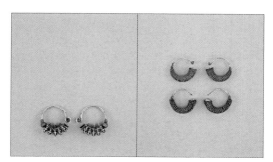
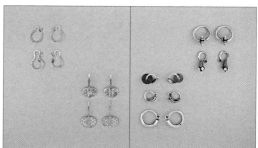

Pages 178-179
China, Guizhou (Miao)
Silver. H. 5.8 and 5 cm
Many open earrings are
kept in place by a spiral at
one end.

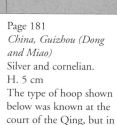

Page 180
*China, above, the island of
Hainan (Miao)*
Silver. H. 5.4 cm
The Miao of Hainan wear
only earrings and
bracelets. Although they
were found in China, the
engraved motifs of the
lower pendants suggest
that they are probably
Meo.

Page 181
*China, Guizhou (Dong
and Miao)*
Silver and cornelian.
H. 5 cm
The type of hoop shown
below was known at the
court of the Qing, but in
jade.

Page 182
China, Guizhou (Miao)
Silver. H. 6.6 cm
The flat spiral,
reminiscent of a coiled
serpent, dates back to
archaic China. The
serpent is closely
associated with the fertility
of the soil, since, like the
seeds themselves, it leaves
the underworld to come
up to the surface in
spring.

Page 183
China (Miao and Dong)
Silver, enamel and
cornelian. H. 6.5 cm
Miao women sometimes
wear several different types
of earrings one on top of
the other.

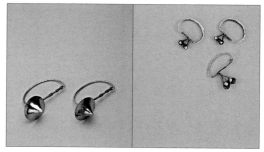
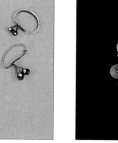

Page 184
China (Dong)
Silver. W. 11 cm
The cones are hollow.
The earrings illustrated in
this double page, as well
as many ornaments
typical of ethnic
minorities, greatly
impress design lovers.

Page 185
China, Guizhou (Miao)
Silver. W. 6.5 cm

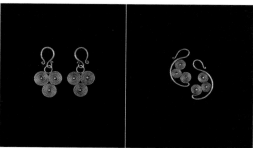

Pages 186-187
China (Miao)
Silver. H. 9.9 cm
and 8.3 cm
The spiral is a motif
dating back to the Bronze
age and the exceptional
variety of shapes recalling
such symbol is really
astonishing. The two
pairs of earrings
illustrated are a pleasantly
harmonious example.

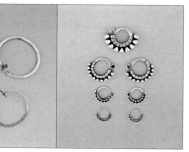

Page 188
China, Guizhou (Miao)
Silver. Diam. 8.8. cm
Rings have always
inspired the creativity of
goldsmiths.

Page 189
China, Guizhou (Miao)
Silver. W. 6.5 cm
Dong women wear these
earrings in their ear lobes.
The upper one is hollow.

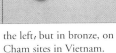

Page 190
China
Silver-gilt. H. 8 cm
Hollow pendants like
those shown here are worn
by women of Han origin.

Page 191
China (Dong)
Silver. H. 8.5 cm
Fruits are often regarded as
symbols of fecundity
because of their many
seeds.

Page 192
China, Guizhou (Miao)
Laos and *Vietnam*, the
spirals
Silver. H. 7 cm
The heavier they are, the
more beautiful such
bobbins are considered to
be. The ear lobe will be
stretched according to
their weight, and the
earrings will tilt forwards.
Archaeologists have found
spirals like those shown on

the left, but in bronze, on
Cham sites in Vietnam.

Page 193
China (Dong)
Silver. Diam. 2.9 cm
These reels have two sides
(bottom left). their filigree
decoration is particularly
fine.

Page 194
China, Guizhou (Miao)
Silver. H. 12 cm

Page 195
China
Silver and engraved jade.
H. 7.2 cm
These ear pendants date
from the period of the
Ch'ing, or Xing, a
Manchu dynasty which
settled in China in1644
and held the power until
1912.

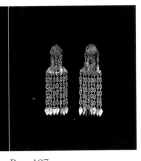

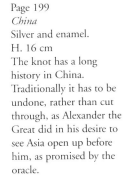
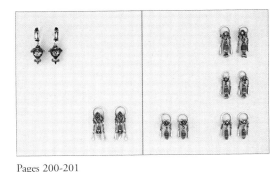

Page 196
China
Silver. H. 16.5 cm
The engraved symbol
visible on the buttons also
figures on textiles and
other gold and silver
objects made by Han
goldsmiths.

Page 197
China, Guizhou (Miao)
Silver. H. 14 cm
Pendants and chains give
an impression of lightness.

Page 198
China (Yao?), Qing period
Silver and enamel.
H. 9 cm
The bat (left) is a symbol
of happiness, sometimes
found in conjunction with
the ideogram for longevity
in the expression of
wishes. There are some
hundred known variants
of the *shou* symbol seen to
the right, which is an
expression of a wish for
long life.

Page 199
China
Silver and enamel.
H. 16 cm
The knot has a long
history in China.
Traditionally it has to be
undone, rather than cut
through, as Alexander the
Great did in his desire to
see Asia open up before
him, as promised by the
oracle.

Pages 200-201
China (Dong)
Silver, enamel, cornelian
and glass. H. 7.5 and
6.5 cm
These outstandingly
refined earrings reflect the
sensibility and ability of
Chinese craftsmen, who
particularly appreciate the
flowers motif.

Page 202
China (Miao)
Silver. H. 6.1 cm
A typical example of the wonderfully inventive silverware produced by the various minorities.

Page 203
Taiwan
Shell and glass beads. H. 7.2 cm
The facets enhance the rather austere shape of these earrings.

Page 204
Mongolia
Silver, enamel and cornelian. H. 11.8 cm
Worn by women in pairs, when they are very long *süike* are attached to the headdress.

Page 205
Mongolia (Chahar)
Silver and coral, H. 25.5 cm
Married women wear these pendants as part of their headdress. *Shiru* coral is particularly prized by the Mongols: its red colour symbolises life, and nomad women are great lovers of colourful materials, according to Boyer.

Page 206
Mongolia
Silver, glass paste, coral and enamel. W. 8 cm.
In the past, hoops of the type shown above were worn around the ear. They have marked similarities with Tibetan jewels, not just in terms of shape, but also in the technique used for the mounting of the stones.

Page 207
Mongolia
Silver, turquoise and coral. H. 11 cm
The technical perfection and the precision of details lead to think that these earrings were made by Chinese craftsmen.

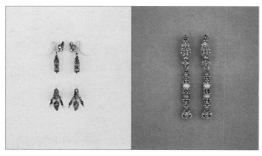 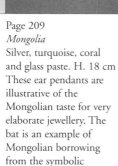  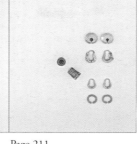  

Page 208
Mongolia (Chahar)
Silver and coral. H. 6.5 cm
As a celestial and creative power, the dragon (above) is a reference to the emperor. Uniting earth and sky, it symbolises the celestial rain bringing fertility to the earth. The cicada (below), which sings in the heat of the day, and falls silent at night, has become the symbol of the twinned ideas of light and darkness.

Page 209
Mongolia
Silver, turquoise, coral and glass paste. H. 18 cm
These ear pendants are illustrative of the Mongolian taste for very elaborate jewellery. The bat is an example of Mongolian borrowing from the symbolic vocabulary of China.

Page 210
Vietnam, the three pairs, and *Thailand, Ban Chiang*
Glass, cornelian and excavated quartz. H. 5 cm
Masters of the art of glassmaking, colonies of Greco-Roman merchants had settled in Arikmedu, in South India, and the technique spread from there to South-East Asia. The large pair of glass earrings are examples of Cham workmanship. The little ones date from the sixth century.

Page 211
Burma, Cambodia and *Vietnam*
Gold, precious stones and silver-gilt sheet (first row to the right).
Diam. 2.5 cm
Group of excavated earrings. The cylinders with fine filigree and rubies date from the Pyu period (X-XI centuries); the split pair are Cham; the others date from the Mon period in Cambodia.

Page 212
Cambodia, Angkor (Khmer)
Bronze. H. 3 cm
This ear ornament is a perfect example of the duality of styles found throughout South-East Asia: the spiral, which dates back to the Bronze Age, and the conch, which is a Hindu symbol.

Page 213
Cambodia
Bronze. H. 6.8 cm
This ornament (10th-12th century) is decorated with a mythical creature, half serpent, half elephant, whose raised trunk and two small tusks are visible here.

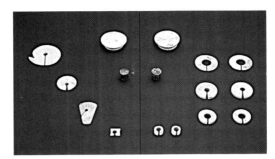

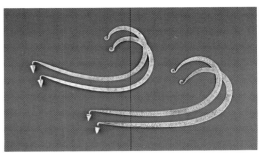

Page 214
Burma (Padaung)
Gold, the three pairs, and partly gilded copper.
H. 5 cm
It is hard to imagine women wearing such refined and delicate earrings as these, with their ornaments in coarse brass wire. The cylinders, which often contain a relic, have ends in the form of *chedi*.

Page 215
Burma, Thailand, Ayuthya, and Cambodia
Gold, silver-gilt and glass.
Diam. 4.4 cm
The hoops and the pair shown to the right, are Burmese; those with hooks Cambodian; the buttons on the left Vietnamese. Those in the centre, and to the right, date from the Ayuthya period.

Pages 216-217
Thailand, Ban Chiang, and Vietnam, Champa
Shell, stone (the group on the right) and terracotta (the small ones in the centre). H. 6 cm, diam. 5 cm
Archaeologists have found a number of stone and shell ornaments in tombs; their extreme hardness and durable character served symbolically to protect the souls of those whom they accompany on their new life. The motif of the open hoop, with a central hole, is a metaphor for the life-giving power of the woman, and was found throughout the South-East Asian mainland and islands until the twentieth century.

Pages 218-219
Golden Triangle (Hmong)
Silver. W. 26 cm
Women wear these ornaments horizontally, attached to their chignons; the studs are worn in the ear lobe as shown in the documents of the Musée de l'Homme photographic archive, dated 1920, gathered by Bernard Dupaigne.

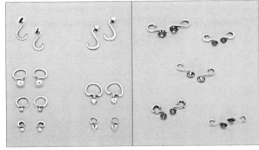

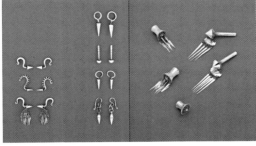

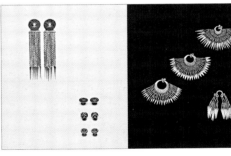

Pages 220-221
Golden Triangle (Hmong)
Silver. H. 5.3 cm, W. 4.5 cm
Meo jewels, made of outstandingly fine silver, are also notable for their clean forms. Whereas rings are very rare, we know of an incredible number of types of earrings, and variations on a single theme. The types shown here had already become rare by the late 1970s.

Page 222
Golden Triangle, Burma and Thailand
Silver. H. 5.4 cm
Hook-shaped earrings are used exclusively by Hmong women. Those ending in a pyramid are Wa. The Bre and Kayah often wear several pairs of inverted cones at a time.

Page 223
Golden Triangle. Burma, Shan State
Silver. H. 10.6 cm
The tapering cylinders and studs are hollow, and may sometimes be of filigree.

Pages 224-225
Golden Triangle, Thailand (Meo)
Silver. H. 12 cm, W. 8.5 cm
The lotus flower and scaled-down torque are recurrent themes. Little triangular rolled gold pieces replace the groups of little ball pendants, formed of two soldered halves, which are popular in India.

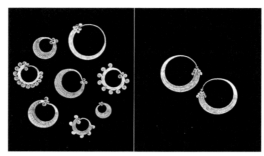

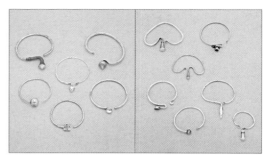

Page 226
Golden Triangle (Akha), Burma, below, *Shan State*
Silver. H. 10.5 cm
Earrings with pendants are also found among the minorities of Yunnan, in China.

Page 227
Golden Triangle (Hmong and Yao)
Silver. H. 6 cm
The earrings shown above left represent the centre of a poppy. The Miao of the island of Hainan also wear trilobate ear pendants; the massive earrings shown top right are characteristic of the Hmong. Those shown below on the right are worn in Laos.

Pages 228-229
Golden Triangle (Meo)
Silver. W. 7.6 and 7.8 cm
The double or sextuple spiral of the terminals is reminiscent of a stylised dragon's head. The execution of the engraved decoration, where any hesitation is fatal, is quite outstanding.

Pages 230-231
Golden Triangle
H. 9.5 and 7.7 cm
Some of these types are also worn by the women of Yunnan, for instance the Dai.

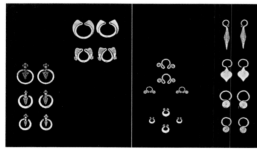

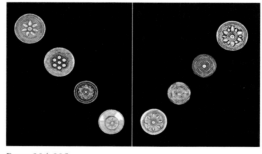

Page 232
Golden Triangle (Yao and Hmong bottom left) and Hmong (above)
Silver and enamel.
Diam. 4.2 cm
The minorities of Vietnam and China also wear earrings with triangular elements. Yao goldsmiths, who also work for other tribes, are highly esteemed.

Page 233
Golden Triangle (Hmong and Lahu, the three pairs below right)
Silver. H. 6 cm
The people of the Golden Triangle set great store by silver jewels, which are easily traded during times of scarcity, new ones being commissioned once the crisis is over.

Pages 234-235
Golden Triangle, frontier region between Burma and China (Sha, Padaung and Akeu)
Silver. Diam. 5.9 cm
Equipped with a long tube for insertion, and decorated in *repoussé*, these ornaments perpetuate the tradition of the buttons of ancient India, and those dating from the Pagan period in Burma.

Pages 236-237
Golden Triangle, Burma
Silver and copper. W. 8.5 and 4 cm
The funnel-shaped pair, and the bands of rolled metal, are Karen; the thickness of these latter is gradually increased in order to stretch the hole in the ear lobe. The upper pair of this group, in the form of a cylinder, imitates the rolled band. Few Chin Laytoo women now wear such bobbin-shaped ornaments (above left, and below). Young

Pa-os males wear the long rolled tubes, while their wives wear the type shown in the group to the right. Bre women wear symmetrical bobbins (above right, and in the centre). The cylinders are Lahu Shi.

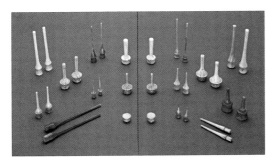

Pages 238-239
Golden Triangle, Burma (Karen)
Ivory. H. 12 cm
By the end of the Seventies it was already rare to see men or women wearing these greatly varied earplugs.

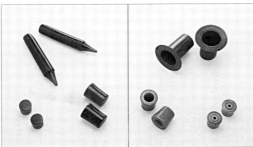

Page 240
Burma (Hkakhu)
Amber. H. 12.5 cm
Elderly women from the Kachin State may still occasionally be seen wearing such amber *patlokan.* This reddish amber, or burmite, was formerly found in deposits in the north of Burma.

Page 241
China and Cambodia
Ivory. H. 6 cm
The making of such funnel-shaped earplugs, the speciality of a Chinese minority, requires immense dexterity. The plugs are generally carved out of the tip of the tusk, which is solid, and polished with the use of dry leaves.

Page 242
Laos and Cambodia
Ivory. Diam. 6 cm
The pattern of the cracks implies that these pairs were carved from the same tusk. The plugs' slightly tapering shape causes them to stay in place. The small conical ones from Cambodia are also used as containers for unguents.

Page 243
Laos and *Vietnam,* the three pairs on the right
Ivory. Diam. 4 cm
Among the minorities of Laos, Cambodia and Vietnam, ivory confers prestige, and is regarded as a sign of wealth.

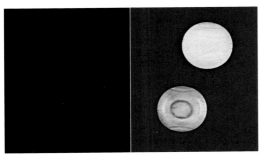

Page 245
Philippines, Mindanao (Bagobo)
Ivory. Diam. 9.5 cm
Only men of high social status may wear the *pamarang.* The button for inserting it into the ear lobe is visible on the earplug below, which is seen from the back.

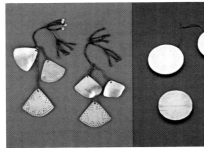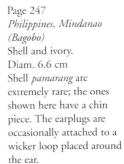

Page 246
Philippines, Mindanao (Bagobo)
Mother-of-pearl, glass beads and brass. H. of each element, 5.5 cm
Women sometimes fix these ear pendants to buttons.

Page 247
Philippines, Mindanao (Bagobo)
Shell and ivory.
Diam. 6.6 cm
Shell *pamarang* are extremely rare; the ones shown here have a chin piece. The earplugs are occasionally attached to a wicker loop placed around the ear.

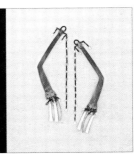

Page 248
Philippines, Luzon (Ifugao)
Mother-of-pearl, Tridacna (Giant Clam) and brass.
H. 11 cm
Spoon-shaped earrings like those shown here are worn by both men and women.

Page 249
Philippines, Luzon (Ilongot)
Hornbill beak, mother-of-pearl and brass. H. 19 cm
Batling are a form of recognition of successful in headhunting, an achievement through which the warrior becomes a full fledged adult, celebrated in poems extolling his manly qualities.

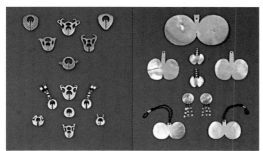

Page 250
Philippines, Luzon (Bontoc, Ifugao and *Kalinga)*
Bronze, silver and gold.
W. 4.5 cm
Dinumug, Lingling-o, set with beads, and *pinangpanga,* with the heads of deer, are variations on the theme of the female genital organs; they are also worn as pendants and necklaces.

Page 251
Philippines, Luzon (Kalinga, Gaddang and *Ilongot)*
Mother-of-pearl and glass beads. W. 12.6 cm
Both Kalinga and Gaddang wear similar *bawisak*; those worn by Kalinga tend to be larger. The discoid pair are an example of Ilongot craftsmanship, whose miniature work is particularly fine.

Page 252
Philippines, Mindanao (T'boli)
Mother-of-pearl, brass and glass beads. H. 16 cm
Repoussé brass discs act as a support for a shower of wonderfully light and graceful mother-of-pearl.

Page 253
Philippines, Luzon (Isneg)
Silver. H. 5.8 cm. End of 17th century.
These earrings may have been inspired by a Mexican model.

Page 255
Indonesia, Java
Gold. H. 4.4 cm
Two juxtaposed styles are seen on earrings found during excavations. One, like this pair, spare and very modern, the other more ornate, comparable with Hindu and Buddhist symbols.

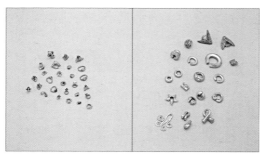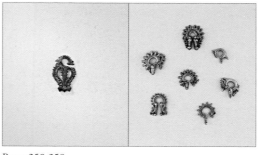

Pages 256-257
Indonesia, Java
Gold and cabochons.
W. 2.1 cm, H. 3.9 cm
These pages illustrate a selection of earrings from the proto-classical period (200 – 700) and the early-classical period (700 – 1000). Several of them have similarities with those of the Philippines, from Oc Eo and Champa in Vietnam, and from Dvaravati in Thailand. The symbolism associated with mount Meru was also adopted in Java,

where high mountains and places were associated with the realm of the spirits. The small earrings on the left, representing the *vajra*, Indra's thunderbolt in the Hindu tradition, are often wrongly referred to as bird rings. Archaeologists have found examples at Uthong, a site dating from the *Dvaravati* period in Thailand. The "V"-shaped pair above dates from the late-classical period (1000-1400).

Pages 258-259
Indonesia, Sumatra (Toba Batak)
Bronze. H. 7.5 and 5 cm
The pendant on the left has acquired a patina as a result of a long period spent underground. Men fix the asymmetrical *sitepal* to their right ear lobe, and the *duri duri* to the left. These ornaments might derive from archaeological models with projections (*duri* means thorn); they play an important part in certain rituals.

Page 260
Indonesia, Sumatra (Karo Batak)
Silver-gilt. H. 8.5 cm
These *raja mahuli* are worn by women.

Page 261
Indonesia, Sumatra (Karo Batak)
Silver-gilt. H. 13.2 cm
Ulang aling, with their long drop earrings, are worn in the outer ear by women and young girls. Aristocratic women wear *padung curu curu* – reminiscent of birds' nests, full of treasures, like attics in the houses of wealthy women – at Adat festivals.

Pages 262-263
Indonesia, Sulawesi, below right, and *Sumatra,* the others
Gold, *suasa,* above left, *intan* diamonds to the right.
W. 4.5 cm, height 5.3 cm
New techniques such as granulation and filigree came in with Islamisation, and were widely used by the Bugis, who were remarkable goldsmiths.

They were also shrewd traders, skilled sailors and builders of magnificent boats, and had trading posts at Sumbawa and Makassar.

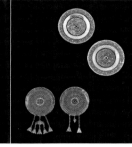

Pages 264-265
Indonesia, Sumatra, the high plateaux of *Padang (Minangkabau)*
Gold and *suasa.* Diam. 10.5 and 7 cm
Such *subang* confirm the reputation of the goldsmiths of Padang, who learned their trade from those of the sultanate of Aceh.
The delicacy of the *repoussé,* filigree and

granulation are quite simply breathtaking.

Pages 266-267
Indonesia, Sumatra (Karo Batak)
Silver. H. 17 cm
These photographs show how women wear *padung padung,* which also reflects the shift in power between men and women. The collection of jewels worn at the wedding ceremony illustrates their complementarity. The key pin visible at the top of

the earrings enables them to be inserted into the lobe; they may also be attached to a headscarf, in order to lighten their considerable weight.

Page 268
Indonesia, Nias
Bronze. H. 8 cm
Sialu, in the form of the tropical laurel are worn by women.

Page 269
Indonesia, Nias
Gold. W. 12.5 cm
Saru dalinga are worn in pairs, by women; men wear a single one, known as a *gaule.* This latter – seen represented on the wooden panels of houses, combined with palm leaves, a female symbol – is a metaphor for the union of the two sexes.

Page 270
Indonesia, Kalimantan. (Kayan Dayak)
Wood. H. 10 cm
At one time, ancient Borneo was divided upon between Malaysia – the northern province – which took on the name Sarawak, Indonesia – where it became Kalimantan – and the sultanate of Brunei, an enclave in Sarawak. *Dayak* means people of the interior, or of the mountain; the adjective specifies the tribe.

Page 271
Indonesia, Kalimantan (Kayan Dayak)
Casque of hornbill. W. 11 cm
Worn by headhunters, in their distended ear lobes. The hornbill is one of the heroes of the Dayak creation myths. Such ornaments, which do not form a pair, have openwork based on a curvilinear *aso* motif. The plate on the earring below shows a seated figure and the face of a mythical creature known as the *aso.*

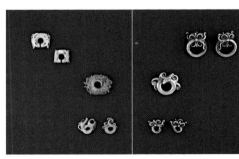

Pages 272-273
Indonesia, Kalimantan (Dayak)
Hornbill beak and bronze. W. 5.5 and 5.1 cm
Such ornaments are worn exclusively by men. The ones in bronze, worn at the height of the collarbone were worn together with panther's teeth; placed in the rim of the ear, they transferred the panther's power to their wearer. The *Aso* is a sort of dragon/serpent with a gaping mouth.

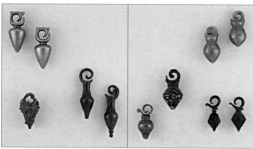 

Pages 274-275
Indonesia and *Malaysia, Kalimantan* and *Sarawak (Dayak)*
Brass, lead, porcelain and wood. H. 10 and 8 cm
These remarkably heavy ornaments are worn on stretched lobes (often reaching the armpits) and are used by several Dayak groups. However this tradition is slowly disappearing and some

women even recur to surgery to close the wounds. The wood pendants are used by women only.

Page 276
Indonesia, Borneo
Silver. W. 7 cm
A rare type of earring.

Page 277
Indonesia, Kalimantan (Dayak)
Bronze and wood. Diam. 6.5 cm
The curvilinear motifs of the wooden plugs may be derived from those found on ceramics of the Chou period (1122-221 B.C.), themselves possibly influenced by the Scythians.

Page 278
Malaysia, Sarawak (Dayak)
Wood inlaid with lead and silver. Diam. 5 cm
Plugs in the shape of a bobbin are a very old type of ear ornament, recorded by Postel in ancient India.

Page 279
Indonesia, Bali (left) and *Malaysia, Sarawak*
Silver. Diam. 6.2 cm
Subeng with a spiral motif also have Indian origins. The ornaments on the right have decoration in the form of a diamond. In the past, Borneo was a producer of grey diamonds.

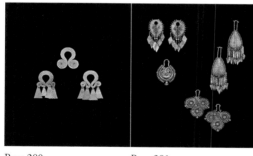 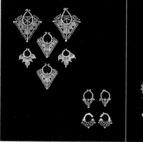

Page 280
Indonesia, Jambi
Suasa. H. 5.8 cm
Here the spiral is one of the motifs inspired by the Dongson culture from Vietnam.

Page 281
Indonesia, Flores (Nage and Lio)
Gold. H. 9.5 cm
Various type of ear pendants from Flores are offered to one another by wealthy families as engagement pledges. The trilobed *tebe* and the *ate saga* are part of the *adat* family treasure, and have a sacred character.

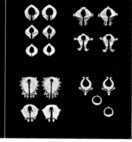

Page 282
Indonesia, Timor
Silver. H. 6.8 cm
Like the travelling goldsmiths from Ndao, a small island near Roti, the Tetum too procured jewels from the Atoni of the coast. *Kawata* earrings and bracelets are lavishly decorated with spirals.

Page 283
Indonesia, Flores (Nage and Ngada) to the left, and small pair to the right, and *Timor*
Silver. H. 4.5 cm
These are variants on the theme of the split earring. Ngada parents offer *bela* (below) – of which versions in gold are found – to their daughters at *adat* ceremonies; the type with lavish granulation would seem to be the older.

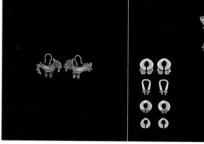

Page 284
Indonesia, Lakor?
Gold. W. 5 cm
Despite their asymmetry, these stylised birds do nonetheless form a pair of ear pendants; indeed, their very differences indicate as much. The nobility of the centre of the island greatly appreciated zoomorphic ornaments. Those in gold are worn exclusively by *raja* chiefs, their families, and the aristocracy.

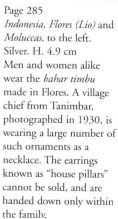

Page 285
Indonesia, Flores (Lio) and *Moluccas,* to the left.
Silver. H. 4.9 cm
Men and women alike wear the *bahar timbu* made in Flores. A village chief from Tanimbar, photographed in 1930, is wearing a large number of such ornaments as a necklace. The earrings known as "house pillars" cannot be sold, and are handed down only within the family.

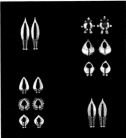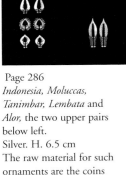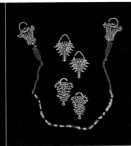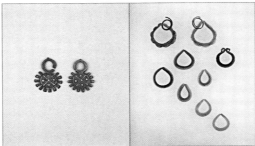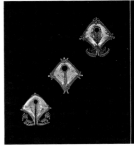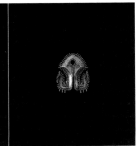

Page 286
Indonesia, Moluccas,
Tanimbar, Lembata and
Alor, the two upper pairs
below left.
Silver. H. 6.5 cm
The raw material for such
ornaments are the coins
obtained over the
centuries during profitable
commercial transactions
with Europeans which are
then melted down and
cast. The elongated

earrings, known as
"crocodiles", are from
Lembata.

Page 287
Indonesia, Moluccas,
Tanimbar
Gold. H. 5.6 cm
Kwene are worn by
women, sometimes linked
by a chinpiece.

Page 288
Indonesia, Tanimbar
Bronze. H. 7 cm
Pepek soriti are worn
exclusively by young girls,
and serve to stretch their
ear lobes.

Page 289
Indonesia, Irian Jaya
Gold and coconut.
H. 6 cm
These earrings, dating
from the Majapahit
period, were discovered
during excavations.

Pages 290-291
Indonesia, East Sumba to
the left, *West Sumba* to the
right.
Gold. H. 7.8 and 8 cm
Mamuli are worn in the
ear, suspended from the
turban or from a chain or
pendant, and are suggestive
of the womb. Simple ones
are given during
matrimonial dealings; the
more complex ones, whose
bases are decorated with

deer or birds, are regarded
as family heirlooms, and
cannot be sold. They
acquire their reddish colour
from the libations made in
the sacrificial blood of
chickens or other small
animals. Stylised horses'
heads – a motif also found
on textiles – figure at the
base of the *pewisie*, to the
right. The local *rajas* grew
rich through trading horses
with the Europeans.

America

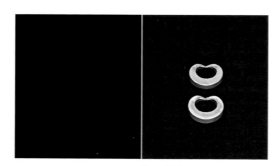

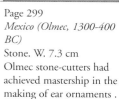

Page 292
Brazil, Amazonia
Wing cases of the *buprestis* beetle. H. 18 cm
The iridescent reflections give this male ornament a magical effect. Despite their apparent fragility, such wing cases are remarkably durable. The slightest movement sets the *pendants* tinkling, and they may serve as an accompaniment to dances.

Page 297
Colombia, Magdalena (Tairona)
Gold. W. 6.7 cm
The Tairona culture reached its peak between the tenth and sixteenth centuries, and the work of Tairona goldsmiths exerted a widespread influence; their preferred techniques being hammering, *repoussé* and the lost wax process.

Page 298
Peru (Chimu, 1200-1400)
Silver. H. 4.1 cm
Birds are a favourite motif among Chimu goldsmiths.

Page 299
Mexico (Olmec, 1300-400 BC)
Stone. W. 7.3 cm
Olmec stone-cutters had achieved mastership in the making of ear ornaments .

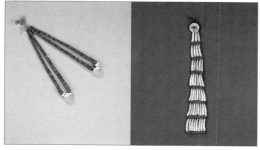
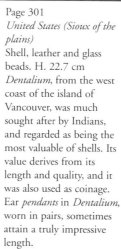

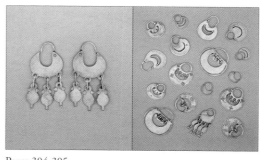

Page 300
United States. (Pueblo)
Turquoise, shell and glass paste. H. 17.5 cm
The women hang *jaclas* from their ears or necklaces. Already used by Indians before the Christian era, turquoise is credited with magical properties; known as 'skystone', it is a symbol of luck, health and happiness.

Page 301
United States (Sioux of the plains)
Shell, leather and glass beads. H. 22.7 cm
Dentalium, from the west coast of the island of Vancouver, was much sought after by Indians, and regarded as being the most valuable of shells. Its value derives from its length and quality, and it was also used as coinage. Ear *pendants* in *Dentalium*, worn in pairs, sometimes attain a truly impressive length.

Pages 302-303
Ecuador (Chocos)
Silver and wood. W. 10.5 cm, H. 8 cm
The earrings to the right are worn by women, those to the left by men.

Pages 304-305
Chile (Mapuche)
Silver. H. 13.7 cm, H. 6 cm
The *chachuay* sometimes have riveted clasps. In the form of a half-moon, they are generally in openwork and decorated with geometrical or floral motifs.

Pages 306-307
Chile (Mapuche)
Silver. H. 6.3 cm,
W. 8.5 cm
The *upul* are made of a
single piece. In the past,
an earring and a stone
pendant were the chief's
only emblems of power.

Page 308
Brazil, Amazonia
Feathers. H. 21 cm
Each tribe has its criteria
as to the choice of the
type and colouring of the
feathers which are its
distinguishing feature.

Page 309
Brazil, Amazonia
(Erikbatsa)
Feathers and porcupine
quills. H. 16 cm

Pages 310-311
Brazil, Amazonia
H. 16 cm, W. 14 cm
The ornament shown
below right is worn by
young Karaja girls.

Pages 312-313
Brazil, Amazonia (Jivaro)
Feathers and bone.
H. 17 cm

Appendix

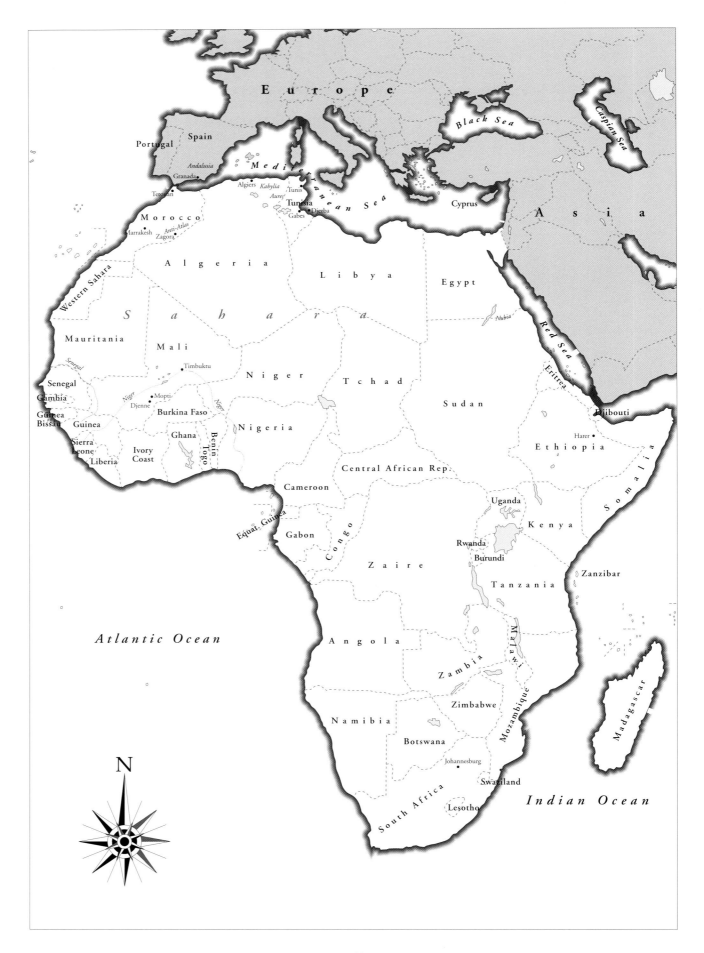

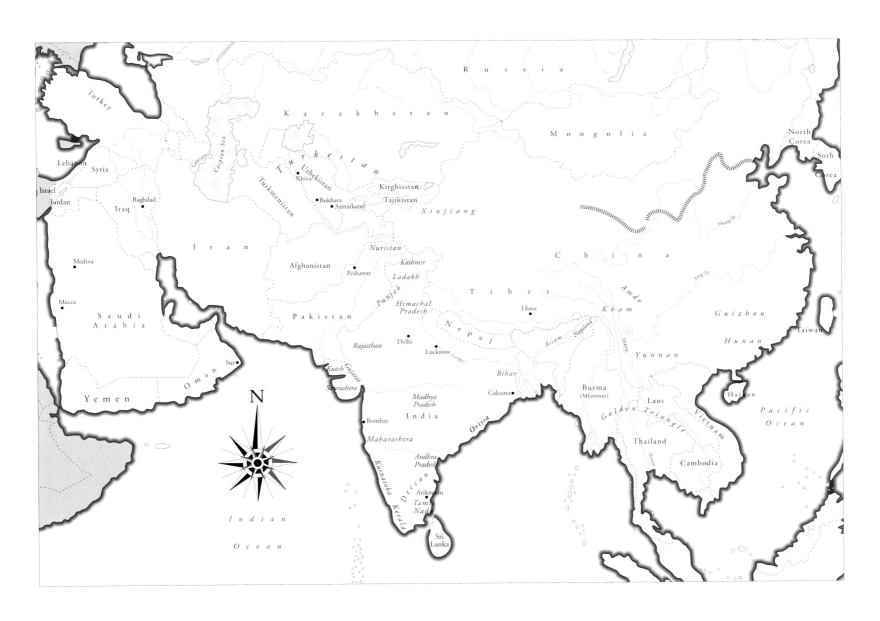

345

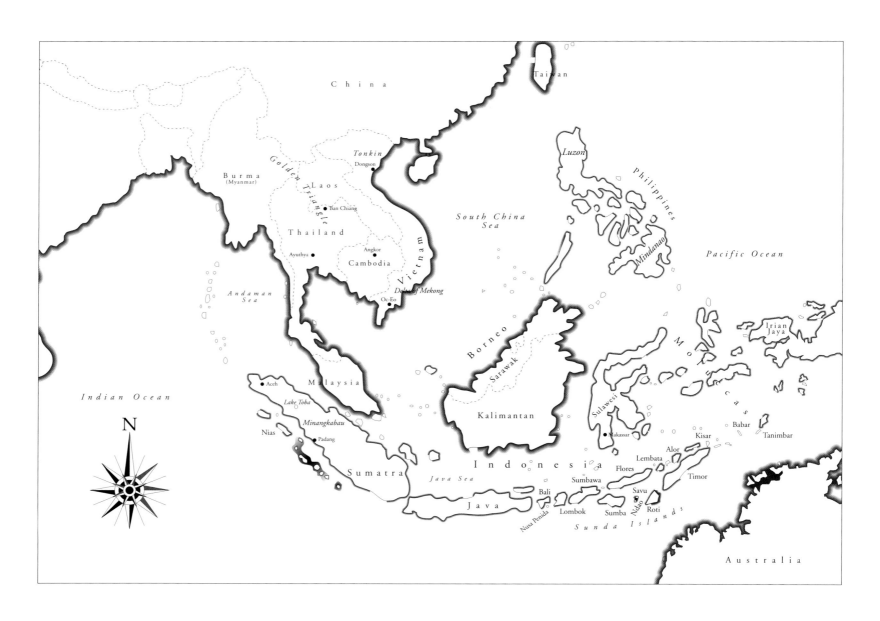

Planes

United States

Mexico

Guatemala

Caribbean Sea

Venezuela

Colombia

Guyana

Suriname

Fr. Guiana

Ecuador

Amazonas

Peru

Brazil

Bolivia

Pacific Ocean

Paraguay

Argentina

Chile

Uruguay

Atlantic Ocean

N

Glossary

Many information included in this glossary have been derived from C. Arminjon et M. Bilimoff, *L'Art du Métal*, Éditions du Patrimoine, 1988

Alloy
A mixture or two or more metals heated to melting point.

Beating
The making of very fine sheets of metal.

Bobbins
Cylinder-shaped earrings decorated with a groove.

Brass
An alloy of copper and zinc of yellow colour.

Bronze
An alloy of tin and copper.

Buttons
Earrings or part of them, ornamenting the lobe. They are made up by a sphere or a little motif and may have a pendant.

Casting
The shaping of a molten metal by pouring it into a mould. Various techniques are used according to the nature and volume of the metal in question, and the number of objects required.

Champlevé
Relief obtained through the removal, by engraving, of more or less extensive areas of the metal, used mainly in *champlevé* enamel.

Chasing
Decoration, with lines and indented surfaces, done on the right side of a metal, in sheet or solid, without removing any material, unlike engraving. It is done using a chasing tool, or tracer, held at right angles to the surface to be hammered; it is cold worked on a soft support, in order that lines and relief may be heightened, or toned down, as required.

Cloisonné
A technique for the applying of enamels in compartments bounded by delicate cells (cloisons), in metal strips or wire, soldered on to a metal base.

Copper
A red-brown metal, ductile and malleable, and a good heat conductor, receptive to treatment with acids; when oxidised in the atmosphere, copper produces verdigris. Either pure or as an alloy, it is worked by hammering. It can only be chased in combination with other metals, its main alloys being bronze and brass.

Draw plate
A metal plate pierced with progressively narrowing holes, through which the wire is passed until it reaches the thickness required.

Earplug
An ornament often of spool shape inserted in the lobe of the ear, especially to distend it.

Earring
An ear ornament with or without a pendant attached to a pierced earlobe by a loop of wire or to an unpierced earlobe by a screw or a clip.

Enamel
A vitreous material composed of a colourless, crystalline mass, the base, and colorants, generally metal oxides.

Enamelling
The various procedures used for the application of an opaque, translucent enamel to a base in gold, silver, copper or their alloys.

Encrustation
The decoration, with metals of a different colour, of a base in metal, or some other material, as in champlevé enamel or niello.

Engraving
Decoration obtained by removing material from a support by means of a sharp tool.

Fake granulation
Decoration imitating granulation, obtained by various stamping techniques.

Filigree
Decoration with gold, silver or silver-gilt wire; singly or in groups, the wires are arranged as the motif requires, fixed and soldered onto a metal base. Soldered to one another, they form an openwork ornament, and may be decorated with granules or pearls.

Forging
The shaping of a metal, generally when it is red hot, worked and forged on an anvil.

Founding
A process which consists of melting down the metal, or the metals making up an alloy, in a crucible, then pouring the liquid metal into a mould.

Gilded silver (or **Silvergilt**)
Silver covered with a thin layer of gold laid on as a gold leaf or otherwise.

Gilding
A thin sheet of gold applied to a metal object.

Gold
A non-corrodible metal, ductile and malleable. It is easily laminated into sheets, stretched into fine wire or cast into granules. It may be *repoussé*, chased, engraved, encrusted, nielloed or enamelled. Because of its relative softness, it is usually alloyed with other metals.

Granulation
Decoration consisting of minute solid spheres, in gold or silver, fixed on to a base in the same metal. It is frequently used together with filigree.

Intan
Indonesian term meaning diamant.

Iron
A malleable metal which can be forged either hot or cold.

Leaf gilding
The gilding of a metal with the application of gold leaf, worked either hot or cold.

Lost wax process
May be either solid, or hollow, in which case it has a central core in some refractory material. The molten metal is then run in to replace the wax model, in a mould which may then be destroyed after casting, once the object has cooled down. If the original model is destroyed, the lost wax process produces a single, unique object.

Matrix
A mould whose imprint permits the making of a number of identical objects.

Mercury gilding
Gilding which uses an amalgam of gold and mercury. Once the amalgam has been applied and heated, the mercury volatilises and the gold spreads to cover the surface to be gilded.

Mounting
The assembling and fixing of stones or other materials in a metal mount

Niello
Inlaid decoration of a blackish material into lines cut away from a light-coloured metal. Niello has a base of metal sulphides.

Openwork
A motif cut out of a sheet of metal.

Pendants
Drop-shaped earrings.

Pokerwork
The application, on ivory, bone or wood, of decoration with the use of a red-hot utensil.

Punching
A kind of ornamental perforation.

Repoussé
A technique for making relief decoration on a metal sheet. The goldsmith works the metal from the back, to make the form stand out; such work is often completed on the front with chasing.

Sand casting
The model, in a hard material, is moulded in refractory sand, packed into a box mould. Sand casting permits the making of a number of identical objects.

Sheet metal
The metal is hammered by the goldsmith into sheets of various thickness, which may then be shaped by a variety of procedures.

Silver
A precious metal, very ductile and malleable, found either in its pure state or in ores, mingled with other metals such as lead, copper or zinc. Sterling silver is made up of 925‰ of silver and 75‰ of copper.

Silvering
A coating of silver applied to a metal object.

Soldering
The joining together of metal surfaces by heating them directly on a fire or by means of a blowlamp. It may be done with or without the use of an easily fused alloy, the solder.

Stamping
A technique for the decoration, in relief, of a sheet of metal by means of a punch, or mould, allowing for the making of multiple copies. The mould, generally of bronze or steel, has an *intaglio* version of the required decoration, which will be in relief, and the process consists of hammering the sheet of metal into the mould. As with *repoussé*, the metal is stamped on the reverse, so as to obtain precise and clear-cut forms in relief on the right side.

Studs
Disc- or cylinder-shaped earrings inserted into a hole pierced in the ear.

Suasa
Indonesian term indicating a gold and copper alloy in which the last element is predominant.

Temporal ornaments
These earrings are worn at temple level, hung to headdresses, usually due to their dimensions and weight.

Wet gilding
The gilding, by immersion, of small objects in silver, copper or brass, based on the principle of the precipitation of metals and of their solution by other more oxidizable ones.

Wire
Metal may be made into wire either by hammering or by drawing through a draw plate. The resulting wires may be of various sections, dimensions and calibres, decorated or otherwise, and assembled in different ways to make or decorate objects.

Index

Bibliography

General

Arminjon C., Bilimoff M., *L'Art du Métal*, Éditions du Patrimoine, Paris 1988.

Borel F., *Le vêtement incarné. Les Métamorphoses du corps*, Calmann-Lévy, Paris 1992.

Borel F., *The Splendor of Ethnic Jewelry*, Harry N. Abrams, New York, 1994. Fr. transl., *Orfèvres lointains. Bijoux d'Afrique, d'Asie, d'Océanie et d'Amérique*, Hazan, Paris 1995. It. transl., *Ethnos. Gioielli da terre lontane*. Skira, Milan 1996. Ger. transl. *Schmuck, Kostbarkeiten aus Afrika, Asien, Ozeanien und Amerika*, Hatje Cantz Verlag, Ostfildern-Ruit 1999.

Chevalier J., Gheerbrant A., *Dictionnaire des Symboles*, Robert Laffont/Jupiter, Paris 1982.

Cerval M. de *et al.*, *Dictionnaire international du Bijou*, Éditions du Regard, Paris 1998.

Gladiss, A. von, *Traditioneller Silberschmuck der islamischen Welt. Aus einer niedersächsischen Privatsammlung*, Kestner-Museum, Hanover 1986.

Hasson R., *Early and Later Islamic Jewelry*, L.A. Mayer Institute for Islamic Art, Jerusalem 1987.

Hasson R., *Schmuck der islamischen Welt. Ausstellung des L.A. Mayer Memorial Museums Jerusalem/Israel*, Museum für Kunsthandwerk Frankfurt/Main 1988.

Hoffmann E., Treide B., *Schmuck früherer Kulturen und ferner Völker*, Kohlhammer, Stuttgart-Berlin-Köln-Mainz 1976. Fr. transl., *Parures des Temps anciens, des Peuples lointains*, Librairie G. Kogan, Paris 1977.

Klever K. and U. *Exotischer Schmuck*, Mosaik, Munich 1977.

Mack J. (ed.), *Ethnic Jewelry*, Harry N. Abrams, New York 1988.

Mascetti D. and Triossi A., *Earrings from antiquity to the present*, Thames and Hudson, London, 1990.

Roy C., *Arts Sauvages*, Robert Delpire, Paris 1957.

Tait H. (ed.), *Jewellery through 7000 years*, The Trustees of the British Museum, London 1976.

Tamisier J.C. (ed.), *Dictionnaire des Peuples. Sociétés d'Afrique, d'Amérique, d'Asie et d'Océanie*, Larousse, Paris 1998.

Africa

Adamson J., *The Peoples of Kenya*, Collins & Harvill Press, London 1967.

Bachinger R., Schienerl P.W., *Silberschmuck aus Ägypten*, Galerie Exler and Co., Frankfurt/Main 1984.

Balandier G., Maquet J. *et al.*, *Dictionnaire des Civilisations africaines*, Fernand Hazan, Paris 1968.

Beckwith C., Fisher A., *African Ark*, Collins Harvill, London 1990.

Benfoughal T., *Bijoux et bijoutiers de l'Aurès, Algérie. Traditions & innovations*, CNRS Éditions, Paris 1997.

Benouniche F., *Bijoux et Parures d'Algérie Grande Kabylie - Aurès*, Ministère de l'Information, Algiers 1982.

Besancenot J., *Bijoux berbères du Maroc*, Galerie de l'orfèvrerie Christofle, Paris 1947.

Böhning W. *et al.*, *Ostafrika. Geräte, Waffen, Schmuck*, Völkerkundemuseum der von Portheim- Stiftung, Heidelberg 1972.

Camps-Fabrer H., *Bijoux berbères d'Algérie*, Édisud, Aix-en-Provence 1990.

Creyaufmüller W., *Silberschmuck aus der Sahara, Tuareg und Mauren*, Galerie Exler & Co., Frankfurt/Main 1982.

Creyaufmüller W., *Völker der Sahara, Mauren und Tuareg*, Linden-Museum, Stuttgart 1979.

Eudel P., *Dictionnaire des bijoux de l'Afrique du Nord*, Ernest Leroux, Paris 1906.

Falgayrettes-Leveau C., *Corps sublimes*, Musée Dapper, Paris 1994.

Fisher A., *Africa Adorned*, Collins, London 1984. Fr. transl. *Fastueuse Afrique*, Éd. du Chêne, Paris 1984. It. transl., *Gioielli africani*, Rusconi Immagini, Milan 1984. Ger. transl., *Afrika im Schmuck*, Du Mont, Köln 1987.

Gabus J., *Au Sahara. Arts et Symboles*, La Baconnière, Neuchâtel 1958.

Gabus J., *Sahara. Bijoux et Techniques*, La Baconnière, Neuchâtel 1982.

Gargouri-Sethom S., *Le bijou traditionnel en Tunisie. Femmes parées, femmes enchaînées*, Édisud, Aix-en-Provence 1986.

Garrard T., *Gold of Africa: Jewellery and Ornaments from Ghana, Côte d'Ivoire, Mali and Senegal in the Collection of the Barbier-Müller Museum*, Munich, Prestel and Geneva, Musée Barbier-Mueller 1989. Fr. transl. *Or d'Afrique, Bijoux et Parures du Ghana, Côte d'Ivoire, Mali et Sénégal de la collection Barbier-Mueller*, Hazan, Paris 1990. Ger. transl., *Afrikanisches Gold: Schmuck, Insignen und Amulette aus Ghana, Mali, dem Senegal und von der Elfenbeinküste*, Prestel, Munich 1989.

Grammet I., De Meersman M. *et al.*, *Splendeurs du Maroc*, Musée royal de l'Afrique centrale, Tervuren 1998.

Kalter J., *Schmuck aus Nordafrika*, Linden-Museum, Stuttgart 1976.

The Local History Museums, *Zulu Treasures: of Kings & Commoners. A Celebration of the Material Culture of the Zulu People*, Kwa Zulu Cultural Museum and the Local History Museums, 1996.

Leuzinger E., *Wesen und Form des Schmuckes afrikanischer Völker*, E. Lang, Zurich 1950.

Musée royal de l'Afrique centrale, *Aethiopia, Objets d'Ethiopie*, Annales, sciences humaines, vol. 151, Tervuren 1996.

Rabaté J. and M-R., *Bijoux du Maroc. Du Haut-Atlas à la vallée du Draa*, Édisud / Le Fennec, 1996.

Ross D.H. *et al.*, *Elephant. The Animal and Its Ivory in African Culture*, Fowler Museum of Cultural History University of California, Los Angeles 1992.

Rouach D., *Bijoux berbères au Maroc dans la tradition judéo-arabe*, ACR Éd., Paris 1989.

Schaffar J.-J., *Trésor et mystère des Berbères du Maroc*, Art World Media, Milan 1990.

Sieber R., *African Textiles and Decorative Arts,* Museum of Modern Art, New York 1972.

Sugier Cl., *Bijoux tunisiens. Formes et symboles*, Cérès Productions, Tunis 1977.

Tamzali W., *Abzim. Parures et bijoux des femmes d'Algérie,* Entreprise algérienne de Presse, Algiers, Dessain et Tolra, Paris 1984.

Asia

Abdullayev P., Fakhretdinova D., Khakimov A., *A Song in Metal. Folk art of Uzbekistan,* Ghafura Guljama, Tashkent 1986.

Baker I., Laird T., *The Dalai Lama's Secret Temple*, Thames & Hudson Ltd., London 2000. Fr. transl., *Le Temple Secret du Dalaï-Lama*, Éditions de la Martinière, Paris 2000.

Bernard P. and Huteau M., *Yunnan-Guizhou. Couleurs tribales de Chine*, Anako Edition, Xonrupt-Longemer, 1989.

Boyer M., *Mongol Jewelry,* Thames and Hudson, London 1995.

Campbell M., *From the Hands of the Hills*, Media Transasia, Hongkong 1978.

Cohen Grossman G. (ed.), *The Jews of Yemen. An Exhibition Organized by the Maurice Spertus Museum of Judaica*, Spertus College of Judaica Press, Chicago 1976.

Casal Father G., *et al.*, *The People and Art of the Philippines,* Museum of Cultural History, University of California, Los Angeles 1981.

Diran R.K., *The Vanishing Tribes of Burma,* Weidenfeld & Nicholson, 1997. Fr. transl., *Birmanie un monde qui disparaît,* Librairie Gründ, Paris 1998.

Dupaigne B., *Le grand art décoratif des Turkmènes,* in "Objets et mondes", vol. XVIII, fasc. 1-2, Paris 1978.

Dupaigne B., *Visages d'Asie*, Hazan, Paris 2000.

Fakhretdinova D., *L'Art de la Joaillerie d'Uzbekistan*, (in Russian), Gafur Gulyam, Tashkent 1988.

Frater J., *Threads of Identity. Embroidery and Adornment of the Nomadic Rabaris*, Mapin Publishing Pvt. Ltd., Ahmedabad 1995.

Gabriel H., *Jewelry of Nepal*, Thames and Hudson, London 1999.

Hawley R., *Omani Silver*, Longman, London-New York, 1978.

Hendley T.H., *Indian Jewellery* (2 vols.), Cultural Publishing House, Delhi 1909, rist. 1984.

Jacobs J. *et al.*, *The Nagas, Hill People of North-East India: Society, Culture and the Colonial Encounter*, Thames and Hudson, London-New York 1991. Fr. transl., *Les Naga – Montagnards entre Inde et Birmanie,* Éditions Olizane, Geneva 1991.

Janata A., *Schmuck in Afghanistan*, Akademische Druck- und Verlagsanstalt, Graz 1981.

Jasper J.E., Pirngadie M., *De Inlandsche Kunstnijverheid in Nederlandsch Indië*, Deel IV, De goud-en zilversmeedkunst, De Boeck & Kunstdrukkerij v/h Mouton & Co., s'Gravenhage 1927.

Kalter J., *Aus Steppe und Oase. Bilder turkestanischer Kulturen,* edition hansjörg mayer, Stuttgart 1983.

Lewis P. and E., *Peoples of the Golden Triangle: Six Tribes in Thailand,* Thames and Hudson, London 1984.

Miksic J.N., *Small Finds: Ancient Javanese Gold,* The National Museum, Southeast Asian Gallery, Singapore 1988.

Miksic J.N., *Old Javanese Gold*, Ideation, Singapore 1990.

Montigny A., *Alliages et Alliances des armes et des bijoux d'Oman*, Institut du Monde Arabe, Paris 1989.

Moor M. De, Kal W. H., *Indonesische sieraden*, Het Tropenmuseum, Amsterdam 1983.

Morris M., Shelton P., *Oman Adorned. A Portrait in Silver*. Apex Publishing, Muscat & London 1997.

Muchawsky-Schnapper E., *The Jews of Yemen. Highlights of the Israel Museum Collection*, Jerusalem 1994.

Munneke R., *Van Zilver, Goud en Kornalijn,* Rijksmuseum voor Volkenkunde, Leyden/Breda 1990.

National Palace Museum (ed.), *Catalogue of the Exhibition of Ch'ing Dynasty Costume Accessories,* Taipeh 1986.

Olson E., *Catalogue of the Tibetan Collection and Other Lamaist Material in the Newark Museum,* vol. IV, Newark, New Jersey 1975.

Postel M., *Ear Ornaments of Ancient India*, Project for Indian Cultural Studies, Bombay 1989.

Rajad J.S., *Silver Jewellery of Oman,* Tareq Rajab Museum, Kuwait 1977.

Richter A., *The Jewelry of Southeast Asia*, Thames & Hudson, London 2000.

Rodgers S., *Power and Gold. Jewelry from Indonesia, Malaysia, and the Philippines from the Collection of the Barbier-Müller Museum Geneva.* Barbier-Müller Museum, Geneva 1985. Fr. transl. *L'or des îles. Bijoux et ornements d'Indonésie, de Malaisie, et des Philippines dans les Collections du Musée Barbier-Mueller,* Geneva 1991.

Ronghui W. *et al.*, *The Chinese national culture of costume and adornment*, China Textile Press, Beijing 1992.

Ross H.C., *Bedouin Jewellery in Saudi Arabia,* Stacey International, London 1978.

Ross H.C., *The Art of Bedouin Jewellery. A Saudi Arabian Profile,* Arabesque Commercial, Fribourg 1981.

Rossi G., *The Dong People of China. A Hidden Civilazation*, Hagley & Hoyle Pte Ltd, Singapore n.d.

Rudolph H., *Der Turkmenenschmuck*, Sammlung Kurt Gull, edition hansjörg mayer, Stuttgart 1984.

Schletzer D. and R., *Alter Schmuck der Turkmenen*, Reimer, Berlin 1983. Engl. transl. *Old Silver Jew-*

ellery of the Turkoman, Reimer, Berlin 1984.

Shizhao K. *et al.*, *Clothings and Ornaments of China's Miao People,* The Cultural Palace of Nationalities, Beijing 1985.

Singer J.C., *Gold Jewelry from Tibet and Nepal,* Thames and Hudson, London 1996.

Srisavasdi B.C., *The Hill Tribes of Siam,* Odeon Store, Bangkok 1966.

Stronge S., Smith N., Harle J.C., *A Golden Treasury. Jewellery from the Indian Subcontinent,* Victoria and Albert Museum and Mapin Publishing, London 1988.

Sychova N., *Traditional Jewellery from Soviet Central Asia and Kazakhstan,* Sovetsky Khudozhnik, Moscow 1984.

Tokhtabayeva S.Z., *Kazakh Jewellery,* FNER, Alma-Ata 1985.

Untracht O., *Traditional Jewelry of India,* Thames and Hudson Ltd., London 1997.

Villegas R., *Kayamanan. The Philippine Jewelry Tradition,* Bangko sentral Ng Philipinas, Manila 1983.

Wassing-Visser R., *Sieraden en lichaamsversiering uit Indonesië,* Volkenkundig Museum Nusantara, Delft 1984.

Weihreter H., *Schmuck aus dem Himalaja,* Akademische. Druck-u. Verlagsanstalt, Graz 1988.

Weihreter H., *Schätze der Menschen und Götter. Alter Goldschmuck aus Indien,* Khyun Edition, Augsburg 1993.

Xianyang Z., *Mœurs et Coutumes des Miao,* Éditions en langues étrangères, Beijing 1988.

Zolla E. and Del Mare C., *Le Vie del corallo. Il corallo nella gioielleria etnica della Mongolia,* Electa, Naples 1997. Engl. transl., *Coral and Mongolian Ethnic Jewelry.*

America

Dubin L.S., *North American Indian Jewelry and Adornment. From Prehistory to the Present,* Harry N. Abrams, Inc., New York 1999.

Fresno Art Museum, *Invisible People: Arts of the Amazon. The Mekler Collection,* Fresno 1992.

Hartmann G., *Silberschmuck der Araukaner,* Chile, Museum für Völkerkunde, Berlin 1974.

Hartmann G., *Gold + Silber. Gold der Kuna, Panama, Silberschmuck der Mapuche, Chile,* Dietrich Reimer Verlag, Berlin 1988.

Instituto de Investigação Cientifica Tropical, *Indios da Amazonia,* Museu de Etnologia, Lisbon 1986.

Lavallée D., Lumbreras L.G., *Les Andes de la Préhistoire aux Incas,* Gallimard, Paris 1985.

Ministère de l'Éducation nationale et de la Culture, *L'or du Pérou. Trésors de l'empire Inca,* Palais des Beaux-Arts, Brussels 1962.

Rautenstrauch - Joest - Museum Köln, *Schätze aus Peru. Von Chavin bis zu den Inka,* Verlag Aurel Bongers, Recklinghausen 1959.

Schoepf D., *et al.*, *L'art de la plume. Indiens du Brésil,* Musée d'ethnographie, Geneva 1985.

Verswijver G., *Kaiapo, Amazonie. Plumes et peintures corporelles.* Musée royal de l'Afrique centrale, Tervuren 1992.